SECRET
RIO DE JANEIRO

T0343581

*Manoel de Almeida e Silva, Marcio Roiter
and Thomas Jonglez*

JONGLEZ PUBLISHING

Travel guides

Manoel de Almeida e Silva was born in the traditional district of Gamboa. As a journalist and education specialist, he has lived in several countries during 28 years of work with the United Nations, but has now settled in Copacabana.

Founder of the Instituto Art Déco Brasil (2005), **Márcio Alves Roiter** is the author of *Rio de Janeiro Art Déco* (Casa da Palavra, 2011), *Art Nouveau e Art Déco: Estilos de Sedução* (Espaço Cultural Península, 2013) and *Um Passeio na História* (with Cynthia Garcia; Arezzo, 2010). Winner of the Cultural Award of the State of Rio de Janeiro, he has organised various exhibitions in Brazil and France, set up the 11th World Congress on Art Deco in Rio in 2011 and acted as a consultant for the restoration of many Art Deco buildings.

Bruno Frederick Toussaint Pereira, a researcher specialising in Rio's architecture and urban planning, recently contributed to *A Construção do Rio de Janeiro Moderno* (Casa da Palavra, 2015), focusing on French architect Joseph Gire, as well as to an inventory of Rio de Janeiro's monuments published by the prefecture in 2015.

Diplomat and mountaineer **Pedro da Cunha e Menezes** has worked for the Environment Secretariat of Rio prefecture and as director of Tijuca National Park. For two years he was deputy representative of Brazil with the United Nations Environment Programme. He has already covered more than 20,000 km of trails in about 500 national parks across 120 countries.

An architect and urban planner who trained in 1976 at the Faculty of Architecture and Urbanism of the Federal University of Rio de Janeiro, where he gained an MA (1998) and PhD (2009) in urbanism, **Carlos Fernando Andrade** has held various administrative functions, such as public works director, Undersecretary of State for Planning, and chair of the State of Rio de Janeiro's National Historic and Artistic Heritage Institute (2011).

We immensely enjoyed writing the *Secret Rio* guide and hope that, like us, you will continue to discover the unusual, secret and lesser-known facets of this city.

Accompanying the description of some sites, you will find historical information and anecdotes to help you understand the city in all its complexity.

Secret Rio also sheds light on the numerous yet overlooked details of places we pass by every day. These details are an invitation to pay closer attention to the urban landscape and, more generally, to view our city with the same curiosity and attention we often feel when travelling …

Comments on this guide and its contents, as well as information on sites not mentioned, are welcome and will help us to enrich future editions.

Don't hesitate to contact us:
E-mail: info@jonglezpublishing.com

p. 252

p. 12

p. 74

p. 116

p. 194

p. 158

p. 220

PETRÓPOLIS, BELO HORIZONTE ↑

TERESÓPOLIS

Campos Elíseos

Santa Maria

São Bento

Santa Tereza

Ilha de Paquetá

Belford Roxo

Ilha do Governador

Duque de Caxias

BÚZIOS

São João de Meriti

✈ **Aeroporto Internacional Rio de Janeiro**

Deodoro

Penha

Ilha do Fundão

Baía de Guanabara

Niterói

Madureira

Ponte Pres. Costa e Silva

Aeroporto Santos Dumont

Meier

MAC de Niterói

RIO DE JANEIRO

Centro

✈

Tijuca

Glória

Foresta de Tijuca

Botafogo

Pão de Açúcar ▲

Jacarepaguá

Copacabana

São Conrado

Ipanema

Barra da Tijuca

Joatinga

Ilha Cagarras

Ilha Comprida

Ilha Rasa

Ilha Redonda

OC...ANO ATLÂNTICO

N

0   5   10 km

CONTENT

Castelo – Praça XV

TIRADENTES' HISTORIC CELL	*14*
MUSEU DO CORPO DE FUZILEIROS NAVAIS	*16*
CENTRO CULTURAL DO MOVIMENTO ESCOTEIRO	*18*
PAINTINGS IN THE NAVE OF IGREJA DE NOSSA SENHORA DA CANDELÁRIA	*19*
BAS-RELIEF OF THE ASSOCIAÇÃO COMERCIAL DO RIO DE JANEIRO (ACRJ)	*20*
THE CHRIST STATUE OF IGREJA SANTA CRUZ DOS MILITARES	*22*
SYMBOLS OF THE PASSION AT IGREJA SANTA CRUZ DOS MILITARES	*24*
SHELL IN THE IGREJA DE NOSSA SENHORA DA LAPA DOS MERCADORES	*26*
STATUE OF ST EMERENTIANA	*28*
GENERAL OSÓRIO'S RIDING GEAR	*30*
SECRETS OF IGREJA DE SÃO JOSÉ	*32*
"AO REI DOS MÁGICOS" BUILDING	*34*
BAS-RELIEFS BY ORESTES ACQUARONE	*36*
GONÇALVES DIAS MEDALLION	*37*
AREZZO'S STAINED-GLASS WINDOW	*38*
SANTA BARBARA E AS OPERARIAS CERAMIC PANEL	*40*
LICEU LITERÁRIO PORTUGUÊS AZULEJOS	*42*
MEDALLION OF EDIFÍCIO BRASILIA	*43*
MUSEU JUDAICO DO RIO DE JANEIRO	*44*
PORTINARI PANELS AT PALÁCIO GUSTAVO CAPANEMA	*46*
CAPANEMA HANGING GARDENS	*48*
GUIDED TOUR OF ACADEMIA BRASILEIRA DE LETRAS	*50*
SANTA LUZIA CAR-PARK WALL	*54*
ART DECO DETAILS OF THE TRIBUNAL REGIONAL DO TRABALHO	*58*
CERAMICS AT THE MINISTÉRIO DA FAZENDA	*60*
STAIRWAY OF THE FORMER MINISTRY OF FINANCE	*62*
IGREJA DE NOSSA SENHORA DO BONSUCESSO	*64*
ESTAÇÃO DE HIDROAVIÕES STAIRCASE	*66*

OVAL PANELS BY LEANDRO JOAQUIM 68
SUGAR LOAVES AT THE NATIONAL HISTORICAL MUSEUM 70
LIBRARY OF THE MUSEU HISTÓRICO NACIONAL 72
BAS-RELIEFS AT THE CENTRO ADMINISTRATIVO DO
TRIBUNAL DE JUSTIÇA 73

Lapa – Centro – Gamboa – Saúde

RARE NEO-EGYPTIAN BUILDING 76
OBSERVATÓRIO DO VALONGO 78
ITAMARATY HISTORICAL AND DIPLOMATIC MUSEUM 80
PALÁCIO EPISCOPAL AND FORTALEZA DA CONCEIÇÃO 82
DI CAVALCANTI FRESCOES ON THE NEWSROOM 86
STATUE OF SÃO DISMAS 88
LAGARTO FOUNTAIN ON RUA FREI CANECA 90
MUSEU DA POLÍCIA MILITAR DO ESTADO DO RIO DE JANEIRO 91
FACADE OF THE FORMER LAMBERT PERFUME AND SOAP
FACTORY 92
MUSEU DA POLÍCIA CIVIL WAXWORKS 94
RIGHT ARM OF NOSSA SENHORA DOS PRAZERES' STATUE 95
RAISED FLOOR OF IGREJA DO SANTÍSSIMO SACRAMENTO
DA ANTIGA SÉ 96
CASA FRANKLIN FACADE 98
MUSEU DA BÍBLIA 99
DI CAVALCANTI PANELS AT THE JOÃO CAETANO THEATRE 100
STATUE OF JOÃO CAETANO 102
GOLDEN ROSE OF THE MUSEU ARQUIDIOCESANO DE
ARTE SACRA 106
AZULEJOS AT THE CLUBE DOS DEMOCRÁTICOS 108
ESCOLA DE MÚSICA CONCERT HALL 110
INVERNO STATUE IN THE PASSEIO PÚBLICO 112
SECRETS OF THE INSTITUTO HISTÓRICO E GEOGRÁFICO
BRASILEIRO 114

CONTENT

Botafogo – Flamengo – Laranjeiras – Catete – Gloria – Sta Teresa

BAS-RELIEF STATUE OF SÃO SEBASTIÃO	118
GETÚLIO VARGAS MEMORIAL	120
MEMORIAL COMMEMORATING THE OPENING OF THE PORTS IN 1808	122
VILLINO SILVEIRA DOORWAY	124
MONUMENT TO THE CARIOCA RIVER	126
GRUTA DE LOURDES, IGREJA DA SANTISSIMA TRINDADE	130
MORRO DA VIÚVA	132
CASA MARAJOARA	136
STAINED-GLASS WINDOWS AT FLUMINENSE FOOTBALL CLUB	138
PALÁCIO GUANABARA	140
GRAVEYARD OF THE "LITTLE ANGELS"	142
TOMB OF THE MARQUIS OF PARANÁ	144
STAINED-GLASS WINDOW COMMEMORATING THE NAVY DEAD	146
PROJETO MORRINHO	148
SOCIEDADE BUDISTA DO BRASIL	150
FORMER VATICAN EMBASSY IN RIO	151
RUSSIAN ORTHODOX CHURCH OF ST ZINAIDA	152
THE REMAINS OF THE SANTA TERESA CABLE CAR	153
FOUNDLINGS' WHEELS, CARMELITE CONVENTO DE SANTA TERESA	154
ACADEMIA BRASILEIRA DE LITERATURA DE CORDEL	156

Copacabana – Urca

NAPOLEON'S LOCK OF HAIR	160
PAVEMENT DEDICATED TO CARLOS DRUMMOND DE ANDRADE	161
MOSAIC BY LYGIA CLARK	162
BIBLIOTECA ESCOLAR MUNICIPAL DE COPACABANA CARLOS DRUMMOND DE ANDRADE	163
IGREJA SANTA CRUZ DE COPACABANA	164
CHACRINHA STATE PARK	165

COPACABANA BATCAVE   166

REMAINS OF MORROS DO INHANGÁ   168

ITAHY BUILDING   170

ITAÓCA BUILDING   174

GUAHY BUILDING   176

LOBBY OF EDIFÍCIO PETRÔNIO   178

OBELISK TO MARK THE WIDENING OF AVENIDA ATLÂNTICA   180

MORRO DA BABILÔNIA HIKING TRAIL   182

STATUE OF CHOPIN   184

STAIRCASE AT THE MUSEU DE CIÊNCIAS DA TERRA   186

INSTITUTO CULTURAL CRAVO ALBIN   190

GUIDED TOUR OF FORTE DE SÃO JOSÉ   192

Ipanema – Leblon – Lagoa – Gavea – Jardim botanico – Humaita

COFFEE ROUTE   196

CAPELA DE NOSSA SENHORA DA CABEÇA   198

STATUE OF THE ORIXÁ OSSANHA   200

ENTRANCE TO THE ACADEMIA IMPERIAL DE BELAS ARTES   202

GÁVEA ROUTE MARKERS   204

ESOTERICISM OF THE BRAZILIAN FLAG   206

OCCULT SIGNIFICANCE OF MORRO DOIS IRMÃOS   208

BUGLE BOY STATUE   210

VASE OF THE TRIUMPH OF GALATEA BY FRANÇOIS GIRARDON   212

PARQUE NATURAL MUNICIPAL DA CATACUMBA TO HUMAITÁ

TRAIL   214

CENTRO NYINGMA DE BUDISMO TIBETANO   216

PARQUE DO MARTELO   218

Joatinga – São Contrado – Barra da Tijuca – West

HANGAR DO ZEPPELIN   222

"SENTA A PUA" MEMORIAL   226

CONTENT

PONTE DOS JESUÍTAS   228

WALLACE FOUNTAIN   229

1ST BATALHÃO DE ENGENHARIA DE COMBATE   230

RUINS OF THE IMPERIAL SLAUGHTERHOUSE   232

PALACETE PRINCESA ISABEL   233

MARKER NUMBER 7 OF THE ESTRADA REAL (ROYAL ROAD)   234

CAPELA MAGDALENA   236

TRANSCARIOCA TRAIL TO THE WILD BEACHES
OF GRUMARI   238

STATUE OF A FOOTBALL PLAYER   240

BUMBA-MEU-BOI HOUSE/MUSEUM   242

MUSEU BISPO DO ROSÁRIO   244

AÇUDE TRAIL   246

TRANSCARIOCA TRAIL, FROM ALTO DA BOA VISTA
TO MESA DO IMPERADOR   248

THE MYSTERIOUS INSCRIPTION ON PEDRA DA GÁVEA   251

Tijuca – São Cristóvão – North

CENTRO MUNICIPAL DE REFERÊNCIA DA MÚSICA CARIOCA
ARTUR DA TÁVOLA   254

OMBRELLINO OF SÃO SEBASTIÃO DOS CAPUCHINHOS   256

MUSICAL SIDEWALKS OF VILA ISABEL   258

THE FACE OF "BELLINI STATUE"   260

BAIRRO SANTA GENOVEVA   262

COLUNA DE PERSEPOLIS   264

ENTRANCE TO RIO ZOO   266

MUSEU DO SAMBA   270

BASÍLICA MENOR DO IMACULADO CORAÇÃO DE MARIA   272

MUSEU DE IMAGENS DO INCONSCIENTE   274

MUSEU DA VIDA   276

GUIDED TOUR OF PAVILHÃO MOURISCO   278

ASSOCIAÇÃO DE FERROMODELISMO DO RIO DE JANEIRO
(AFERJ)   282

TREM DO SAMBA   284

MONTE ESCADA DE JACÓ   286

IGREJA DO BOM JESUS DA COLUNA   288

MARGAY CAT STATUE   290

CEMITÉRIO DOS PÁSSAROS   292

TUNNELS AND CAVES OF PARQUE DARKE DE MATTOS   294

ALPHABETICAL INDEX   296

Castelo – Praça XV

1. TIRADENTES' HISTORIC CELL — 14
2. MUSEU DO CORPO DE FUZILEIROS NAVAIS — 16
3. CENTRO CULTURAL DO MOVIMENTO ESCOTEIRO — 18
4. PAINTINGS IN THE NAVE OF IGREJA DE NOSSA SENHORA DA CANDELÁRIA — 19
5. BAS-RELIEF OF THE ASSOCIAÇÃO COMERCIAL DO RIO DE JANEIRO (ACRJ) — 20
6. THE CHRIST STATUE OF IGREJA SANTA CRUZ DOS MILITARES — 22
7. SYMBOLS OF THE PASSION AT IGREJA SANTA CRUZ DOS MILITARES — 24
8. SHELL IN THE IGREJA DE NOSSA SENHORA DA LAPA DOS MERCADORES — 26
9. STATUE OF ST EMERENTIANA — 28
10. GENERAL OSÓRIO'S RIDING GEAR — 30
11. SECRETS OF IGREJA DE SÃO JOSÉ — 32
12. "AO REI DOS MÁGICOS" BUILDING — 34
13. BAS-RELIEFS BY ORESTES ACQUARONE — 36
14. GONÇALVES DIAS MEDALLION — 37
15. AREZZO'S STAINED-GLASS WINDOW — 38
16. *SANTA BARBARA E AS OPERARIAS* CERAMIC PANEL — 40
17. LICEU LITERÁRIO PORTUGUÊS *AZULEJOS* — 42
18. MEDALLION OF EDIFÍCIO BRASILIA — 43
19. MUSEU JUDAICO DO RIO DE JANEIRO — 44
20. PORTINARI PANELS AT PALÁCIO GUSTAVO CAPANEMA — 46
21. CAPANEMA HANGING GARDENS — 48
22. GUIDED TOUR OF ACADEMIA BRASILEIRA DE LETRAS — 50
23. SANTA LUZIA CAR-PARK WALL — 54
24. ART DECO DETAILS OF THE TRIBUNAL REGIONAL DO TRABALHO — 58
25. CERAMICS AT THE MINISTÉRIO DA FAZENDA — 60
26. STAIRWAY OF THE FORMER MINISTRY OF FINANCE — 62
27. IGREJA DE NOSSA SENHORA DO BONSUCESSO — 64
28. ESTAÇÃO DE HIDROAVIÕES STAIRCASE — 66
29. OVAL PANELS BY LEANDRO JOAQUIM — 68
30. SUGAR LOAVES AT THE NATIONAL HISTORICAL MUSEUM — 70
31. LIBRARY OF THE MUSEU HISTÓRICO NACIONAL — 72
32. BAS-RELIEFS AT THE CENTRO ADMINISTRATIVO DO TRIBUNAL DE JUSTIÇA — 73

TIRADENTES' HISTORIC CELL

One of Brazil's most significant but least-known historical sites

Hospital Central da Marinha, Ilha das Cobras
Open on request Monday to Friday 9am–1pm
At the far end of Rua Primeiro de Março (left of Rio 450 tunnel),
walk through the military zone as far as Arnaldo Luz bridge and take
the elevator at the Hospital Central da Marinha (Military Hospital), the
entrance to which is opposite the elevator exit

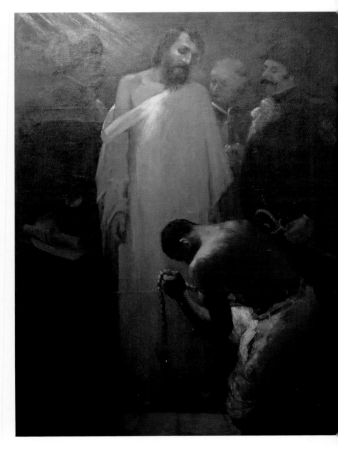

Tiradentes' cell is probably one of Rio's greatest secrets. And yet there's absolutely no indication that it still exists inside the Military Hospital on Ilha das Cobras (Isle of the Snakes) in Guanabara Bay.

Yet any morning, from Monday to Friday, you can simply turn up at the hospital entrance and ask to see the cell. Tiradentes was held prisoner there before being transferred to the city's civilian prison (Cadeia Velha), near the current home of the Legislative Assembly of Rio de Janeiro. It was from this prison, demolished in 1922, that the 45-year-old Tiradentes was led to his execution on 21 April 1792 at the junction of Rua Senhor dos Passos and Avenida Passos, not far from what is now Praça Tiradentes (then Campo da Lampadosa). He was hanged, drawn and quartered, and his head displayed on a pillar in the central plaza of Vila Rica (Ouro Preto). His remains were then scattered at Cebolas, Varginha do Lourenço, Barbacena and Queluz, the towns where he'd called for rebellion against the Portuguese colonial power.

Considered a leading member of the revolutionary movement Inconfidência Mineira (see p. 83), Tiradentes was captured on 10 May 1789 in Rua dos Latoeiros (now Rua Gonçalves Dias) while he was expounding his revolutionary ideas on the independence of Brazil.

The cell of three other Inconfidência Mineira members can also be seen at the Morro da Conceição fortress (see p. 82).

MUSEU DO CORPO DE FUZILEIROS NAVAIS

Yes, you can visit the Isle of the Snakes!

Ilha das Cobras
Tuesday to Friday 9.30am–4.30pm approximately, also last
weekend of the month 1pm–3pm (in which case the military bus departs
from the Naval Museum near Praca XV)
Confirmation by phone recommended: (21) 2126-5053
Guided tours
At the far end of Rua Primeiro de Março (left of Rio 450 tunnel),
walk through the military zone as far as Arnaldo Luz bridge and take
the elevator at the Hospital Central da Marinha. Follow the only road on
the right that leads down and turns left. The entrance is on the left, just past the
military prison
No flip-flops, and bring a passport or identity card

Despite what you might think, you can officially visit Ilha das Cobras (Isle of the Snakes), home of the Brazilian Navy.

You don't need to ask permission, just cross the bridge to the island and climb the steps (or take the impressive elevator) to the highest point and you'll be rewarded with unparalleled views of the city and the island itself.

A three-minute walk along the only road will bring you to the Marine Corps Museum, the official excuse to visit the island.

The museum at the historic site of the fort of São José da Ilha das Cobras is a chance to visit what has been the naval headquarters since the Cayenne military operation in French Guiana ended in 1809. On his arrival in Brazil, King Joao VI was minded to punish the French for invading Portugal by taking over French Guiana, which was the scene of heavy fighting before the Brazilian victory of January 1809. The Brigada Real da Marinha (Royal Naval Brigade, renamed the Marine Corps) reached Brazil with the royal court of Portugal in 1808.

Apart from various objects associated with the marines, the museum's main attraction is a tour of several underground passages (one almost 200 m long) dating from the colonial era. They were built by the Portuguese to get around safely on an island that occupied a strategic position, controlling Guanabara Bay.

Note also the memorial to marines lost in combat: the roof illustrates the sky of 7 March 1808, the date of Joao VI's arrival in Rio. Each of the 162 stars represents 10 of the 1,622 marines killed.

CENTRO CULTURAL
DO MOVIMENTO ESCOTEIRO

Brazilian Scouting museum

Rua Primeiro de Março
(21) 2233-9338
Monday to Friday 10am–5pm
Metro: Uruguaiana

Quite forgotten on Rua Primeiro de Março, not far from the Candelária, the Cultural Center of the Scout Movement is a small museum devoted to the history of Brazilian Scouting. Over the two floors of exhibits, you'll learn that Scouting started in Brazil in 1910 thanks to Amélio Azevedo Marques, and see some interesting old posters and various other items relating to the Scout movement founded by Robert Baden-Powell in 1907.

The origin of the movement goes back to the defence of Mafeking, the British military outpost in South Africa during the Second Boer War (1899–1902): army officer Baden-Powell managed to save the town after a seven-month siege by a much larger enemy force. During that time, Baden-Powell had trained the Mafeking youth as messengers, observers, sentries and scouts.

AINTINGS IN THE NAVE
④
F IGREJA DE NOSSA SENHORA
A CANDELÁRIA

1e church that owes its existence to a storm

ça Pio X
) 2233-2324
nday to Friday 7.30am–4pm, mass on Sunday at 10.30am
tro: Uruguaiana (Presidente Vargas exit)

Although consecrated in 1811, the Church of Our Lady of Candelária was not completed until the late 19th century. Dating from the last decades of that century, the six beautiful paintings on the ceiling of central nave are often overlooked by visitors. The paintings depict the gotten story of the founding of the church in the 17th century. A Spancouple (Antonio Martins Palma and Léonor Gonçalves) were sailing m Europe to Rio on board the *Candelária* when the ship was struck by readful storm. Fearing for their lives, they swore to Our Lady of Canária that they would build a chapel in her honour if they survived. Once ely in Rio they kept their vow and had a chapel built where Candelária rch now stands. The six panels covering the ceiling from entrance to ne show the voyage of the founders, the violent storm and the blessing he original chapel. Unlike other paintings in the church, these are not pired by stories from the Bible. The panels were designed by Brazilian nter João Zeferino da sta (1849–1916) who ght at the Academia perial de Belas Artes peperial Academy of e Arts, see p. 202) and considered to be his sterpiece.

Taking Avenida Presidente Vargas as their point of reference, some people believe the church was built with its back to the city. But in he colonial era it was common for buildings to face Guanabara Bay, he city's main arrival point. Recent revitalisation efforts at the port f Rio de Janeiro have renewed this geographical connection to the ay, highlighted by the demolition of the elevated roadway that once inked the church to the shore.

BAS-RELIEF OF THE ASSOCIAÇÃO COMERCIAL DO RIO DE JANEIRO (ACRJ)

The riches of Brazil carved in stone

Casa do Empresário
Rua Candelária 9
acrj.org.br
(21) 2514-1229
Monday to Friday 9am–5pm
Admission free
Bus: 457, 456, 455, 306, 254

trolling through the historic centre of Rio, it's easy to miss the
beautiful bas-relief in the entrance hall of the Trade Association of
de Janeiro (Casa do Empresário – House of the Entrepreneur), at
junction of Candelária and Buenos Aires streets. Visit the building
ring office hours to admire this 12 m wide and 7 m high bas-relief
itled *Riquezas do Brasil* (Riches of Brazil), sculpted by French artist
ert Freyhoffer. At the centre stands the imposing image of Mercury,
Roman god of commerce, on a base that features the Brazilian flag
tto, *Ordem e Progresso* (Order and Progress). The panel evokes pro-
ction and trade while also highlighting the region's exuberant tropical
a and fauna.

The fifteen-storey building, also known as the Palácio do Comércio,
designed by architects Henri Sajous and Auguste Rendu and opened
May 1940. Its three terraces have panoramic views of Guanabara Bay.
Before acquiring its own headquarters in 1940, the ACRJ had six
porary homes. A year after the arrival of the Portuguese royal fam-
in 1809, the prince regent Dom João expressed his willingness to
struct a commercial square where "merchants could meet, conduct
sactions and handle their business affairs". In 1820, Praça do Comér-
was inaugurated in the premises now known as Casa França-Brasil
ance-Brazil House), close to its present location. It adopted the name
ociação Comercial do Rio de Janeiro in 1867.

Besides reproducing the association's coat of arms in the same
hall, Freyhoffer designed another bas-relief (2.98 m wide and
.47 m high) on the terrace. It shows the god Mercury in the
foreground, flanked by two muses. Both the terrace and the mu-
al are closed to visitors. You can, however, enjoy fine panoramic
views over Guanabara Bay from the 13th floor restaurant.

THE CHRIST STATUE OF IGREJA SANTA CRUZ DOS MILITARES

A miraculous Christ

Rua Primeiro de Março – (21) 2509-3878
Monday to Friday 9am–4pm, mass on Monday, Wendesday, Friday and Saturday at 12pm

In the Rococo church of the Military Holy Cross, consecrated in 18 a sculpture of Christ stands behind the main altar. Although, curic ly, no information is supplied for visitors, this Christ is revealed to miraculous, as Augusto Maurício recounts in *Templos Históricos de de Janeiro*, 1845: "*At some point, Portuguese workman Augusto Frede Corrêa, seeing an image of the dead Christ on the altar, challenged and sulted him. Warned by his workmates, he replied that he had no fear of (and that 'this thing' was just a lump of wood, with no more significance th that. He would only believe in the existence of Christ if he was killed by A at three o'clock that day. Work went on and nobody thought much about u had just happened. But the instant the clock chimed three, a piercing cry heard from the church. The workman, seized by horrible convulsions, had lapsed in front of the altar of Nossa Senhora das Dores (Our Lady of Sorro*

was taken to his home at 48 Rua do Senado, where he lay unconscious three days. On 1 August, however, he was found completely healed, with image of Our Lady of Sorrows clutched in his arms. The whole city was n aware of these events and on the 12th of the same month, Bishop Dom noel do Monte Rodrigues de Araújo went to the scene of the transgression to one prayers in response to the offence given to the statue of Christ. Augusto derico Corrêa, on his knees, begged forgiveness for his contempt, expressing faith and his regrets."

oday, the pardon of the dead Christ is celebrated every 29 July, in memory of the church's statue of Christ, which is placed next to the main altar on that day.

While the present church was being built, bones from the old cemetery were stored in drawers, which would explain why deceased marshals and generals are sometimes heard wandering around the passages. Other than hearing footsteps and voices, many people have claimed that the church organ was playing by itself. In 1923, a fire broke out for no obvious reason on the main altar and rapidly spread, heralding great disaster. Miraculously, the fire went out at the feet of the statue f Nossa Senhora da Piedade (Our Lady of Piety).

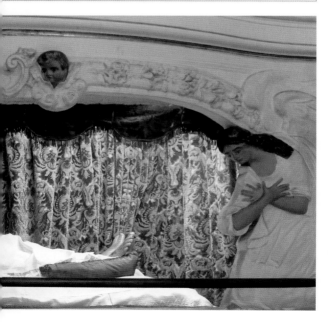

SYMBOLS OF THE PASSION AT IGREJA SANTA CRUZ DOS MILITARES

Rare representation of the symbols of Christ's Passi

Rua Primeiro de Março
(21) 2509-3878
Monday to Friday 9am–4pm, mass on Monday, Wendesday, Friday and Saturday at 12pm

t's easy to visit the attractive church of the Holy Cross of the Military without noticing that the choir contains some very rare and lovely as-reliefs of the instruments of Christ's Passion.

The following are depicted on both sides of the choir: the inscription INRI ("Jesus of Nazareth King of the Jews"); the crown of thorns; the sword with which Peter cut off the ear of the high priest's servant Malchus and the lantern that enabled him to recognise Christ in the arden of Gethsemane; the chalice that collected the blood of Christ which became the Holy Grail); the tunic for which the Roman soldiers rew dice; the rope used to hoist Christ onto the Cross; the lance of the centurion Longinus that pierced his side (see *Secret Rome* in this ries of guides); the jug of vinegar used to moisten his lips; the hammer to drive in the nails and the tongs to pull them out; the ladder for the descent from the Cross; the column where Christ was attached for ourging; the cock that crowed at Peter's betrayal; the long pike with the bile-soaked sponge; the thonged whip; the three nails; and the purse containing the coins of Judas' treachery.

Of the instruments of the Passion most frequently depicted around the world, the only ones missing here are a hand sometimes used to mbolise Pontius Pilate; a skull evoking the place of execution, Golgoa (gulgota is Aramaic for "skull"); and a sun recalling that at Christ's eath there was a solar eclipse lasting three hours.

Veronica's veil, an extraordinary relic

On the wall at the entrance to the choir, to complement the instruments of the Passion, you'll find an image of the face of Christ that isn't particularly striking. Yet this depicts Veronica's veil, an extraordinary and little-known Christian relic which is believed to be an acheiropoietic picture (which means not made by the hand of man).

Above the entrance door, on the street, the inscription *indulgencia plenaria quotidiana* recalls that since 15 April 1923, following a rare privilege, indulgences granted at St Peter's in Rome are also granted to those who come to pray in Santa Cruz dos Militares.

Repeated on the wooden doors of the church are the main instruments of the Passion: the hammer and tongs, together with the crown of thorns and the three nails.

SHELL IN THE IGREJA DE NOSSA SENHORA DA LAPA DOS MERCADORES

Statue hit by a shell

Sacristy, Igreja de Nossa Senhora da Lapa dos Mercadores
Rua do Ouvidor 35
(21) 2509-2339
Monday to Friday 8am–2pm
Metro: Uruguaiana

There's an unexpected sight in the sacristy of the Traders' Church of Our Lady of Lapa – a shell embedded in the wall.

During the 1893 armed forces mutinies against the Brazilian government, a shell fired by the battleship *Aquidabã* hit the church tower and killed the statue that now stands in the sacristy, next to the shell.

Despite falling over 25 m, the statue wasn't greatly damaged: only a few fingers of the left hand were broken off plus a piece of the base, which was recovered and repaired.

Many people regarded this as a miracle, and some still attend church today to pray and petition "Our Lady of the Grotto" on the strength of this incident.

The cult of Nossa Senhora da Lapa is attributed to another alleged miracle that took place in Portugal during the Muslim occupation of the Iberian peninsula. The story goes that the nuns of a convent in the parish of Quintela were afraid of the Moors and fled, hiding an image of Our Lady in a small cave among the rocks. Years later, a young mute girl recovered her speech when she stumbled on the hidden statue. A chapel was built at the site and the cult of Nossa Senhora da Lapa was born.

Back in Rio, a group of merchants who worshipped the same saint at an oratory in Rua dos Mercadores decided to have a church built in 1747. The work took until 1771 and it wasn't until 1812, when the original oratory was demolished, that the statue of Nossa Senhora da Lapa was transferred to the new church. This church, in its current form, is the result of the great reform of 1870 that transformed it into an exemplary harmonious blend of the Baroque and neoclassical. Around this time a tower was added, together with the sculpture that was damaged shortly afterwards. The tower was rebuilt in 1895 and the city's first belfry installed there.

Rua do Ouvidor, originally known as Desvio do Mar in 1578, has since gone through approximately 20 different names. The most recent dates from 1745, when an *ouvidor* (mediator) was working in the locality with the task of listening ("ouvir" in Portuguese) to people's complaints and bringing them before the king.

STATUE OF ST EMERENTIANA

A rare image of the great-grandmother of Jesus

Igreja de Nossa Senhora do Carmo
Rua Primeiro de Março
(21) 2242-4828
Monday to Friday 8am–4pm, Saturday 8am–11am

To the right of the choir of the magnificent church of Our Lady
Mount Carmel, an unobtrusive statue is easily missed. The work
an anonymous 18th-century artist, it is a rare representation of St Eme
entiana, the great-grandmother of Jesus, according to apocryphal texts. I
careful not to confuse her with another St Emerentiana (or St Emerenti
martyred in the 4th century AD.

With her right arm Emerentiana is holding St Anne, and her left ar
supports her daughter, mother of the Virgin Mary. Mary herself hol
Jesus in her arms.

St Anne is shown slightly larger than Mary, perhaps indicating her niority over her daughter. The rich clothes of the different characters dicate their noble and sacred origin.

A stained-glass window at Sainte-Anne-d'Auray church in Brittany (France) also features St Emerentiana.

How do we know about St Emerentiana?

Most of the information on St Emerentiana, who is not mentioned in the Bible, comes from several sources. First are the mystical visions of St Colette of Corbie (1381–1447), Anne-Catherine Emmerick (1774–1824) and Maria Valtorta (1897–1961). Other sources are Paul Victor Charland's *Le Culte de Saint Anne en Occident* (*The Cult of Saint Anne in the West*), published in 1920, and *La vie et les gloires de sainte Anne, tirées d'auteurs anciens et modernes* (*The Life and Glories of Saint Anne, from Ancient and Modern Authors*). Note that Anne and Joachim (parents of the Virgin Mary) are not mentioned in the canonical Gospels: they only appear for the first time in the *Protevangelium* of James, an apocryphal "pre-Gospel" of the 2nd century AD. St Cyril of Alexandria, in the 5th century, picked up this information before The Golden Legend (a 13th-century collection of hagiographies by Jacobus de Voragine) spoke of a sister of Anne's, thought to have been called Hismarian, the mother of Elizabeth and thus the grandmother of St John the Baptist. According to these sources, Emerentiana was born in the village of Sepphoris (Saphora), north of Mount Carmel, where she used to go and meet the disciples of the prophets Elijah and Elysium. It was also on Mount Carmel that Elijah built a chapel dedicated to the Virgin who was supposed to bear a child. Among these disciples was a certain Archos, with whom she regularly kept the mysteries of the faith, who prophesied that she would marry and give birth to the woman who was to be the mother of Christ. At the age of 18, Emerentiana married Stolan, a man of royal blood, who gave her a daughter whom she named Hismarian. When this daughter reached the age of 15, she married Eliud. They had a daughter named Elizabeth, who became the wife of the high priest Zacharias and mother of John the Baptist. Hismarian also gave birth to a child named Emin, who counted among his descendants St Servatius, the first bishop of Tongeren. The years passed and it was only at an advanced age that Emerentiana and Stolan saw themselves fulfil the prophecy of Archos. One day, in a mystical vision, they saw at the head of their bed four golden letters forming the name of Anne, who was born not long afterwards.

GENERAL OSÓRIO'S RIDING GEAR

Why the bootless statue?

Praça XV de Novembro 8
Metro: Carioca

you look closely, you'll notice that the grand equestrian statue of
General Osório in the middle of Praça XV (see below) features him in
dinary dress shoes rather than his usual boots. But there's an explana-
n for this apparent "error".

After researching this commission, sculptor Rodolfo Bernardelli
ose suitable clothes and accessories: a uniform and riding boots. After
mpleting the model, which is kept at the Historical Museum (not
public display), Bernardelli showed it to Osório's daughter, who ex-
ined that her father hadn't worn boots since 1866. During the battle
Passo da Pátria, after 24 hours of torrential rain, the general's legs had
elled so much he couldn't get his waterlogged boots off. He ordered
m to be cut off so he could get back to the fray. He won the bat-
, but subsequently suffered from a leg inflammation that meant he
uldn't wear boots for the rest of his life. After listening to the daugh-
's tale, Bernardelli decided to stick to historical reality and depicted
general in dress shoes rather than riding boots.

The monument was unveiled under the Republic as a tribute
a general of the Empire. It was well received because Osório was
atly appreciated. Public contributions helped to fund this work
d some 40,000 people took part in the inauguration ceremony on
November 1894.

The battle of Passo da Pátria and the famous battle of Tuiuti –
Osório's great military feats in the Paraguayan War – are shown in
two bas-reliefs on the base of the statue. The one pictured (8 m high
and weighing 5,700 kg) was cast in Paris by Ateliers Thibaut in 1892,
from the bronze of cannons captured from the Paraguayans.

Manuel Luiz Osório

Manuel Luís Osório – general, member of parliament, senator, baron,
count and Marquis of Erval – was born in the Brazilian state of Rio
Grande do Sul in 1808. A hero of the Paraguayan War (1864–1870),
he died in Rio in 1879, at his home at what is now number 303
Rua de Riachuelo. His last residence was converted into a museum
n 1983 and is now the home of the Academia Brasileira de Filosofia
(Brazilian Academy of Philosophy). The house, listed as national heritage, is clad with Portuguese *azulejos*.

SECRETS OF IGREJA DE SÃO JOSÉ

A saintly surprise

Avenida Presidente Antônio Carlos
(21) 2533-4545
Monday to Friday 8am–12pm and 2pm–5pm, Sunday 8.30am–11am

On weekday lunchtimes at St Joseph's, you'll notice strange queues among the congregation on the right of the church, deep in the choir. One by one, after waiting patiently, the worshippers disappear behind the altar and reappear moments later.

Visitors have to stand in line like everyone else and venture behind the altar to admire or pray before a spectacular sculpture of the last moments of the life of Joseph, with Mary standing at the bedside of recumbent Joseph, who looks grizzled and defeated, and Jesus at his other side raising a hand in blessing.

The faith demonstrated by believers, as well as the quality and realism of the carving, make this a brief encounter (don't linger in front of the statues, given the number of people waiting), one of intimacy and intense reverence.

Although the 1842 interior is a typical late Rococo work, the original church was built on this same site in the 16th century by the hermit Gas Muniz. In 1659, the city's most sacred relics were moved so that the congregation didn't have to face the gruelling climb to attend the original cathedral on Morro do Castelo (Castle hill). St Joseph's took in the baptismal font, the tabernacle and the patron saint of the city.

The sound of the church bells is famous, thanks to an 1883 carillon that plays a range of tunes.

"AO REI DOS MÁGICOS" BUILDING

A neo-Egyptian building where Brazil's first phone call was made

Rua do Ouvidor 116
Metro: Carioca

here was a time when the streets of Rio were graced with eclectic buildings of various "neo-styles" to give it a cosmopolitan image: manesque, Gothic Revival, neo-Baroque, neo-Rococo, neo-Persian, o-Moresque and neo-Egyptian.

At the junction of Avenida Rio Branco and Rua do Ouvidor is a rticularly striking neo-Egyptian building with two statues of Egyptian vants holding up amphorae of incense on its second-floor balcony. e railings are decorated with winged scarabs and the fourth floor has hed balconies that rear upwards and outwards.

This building, dating from the 19th century before the opening of enida Rio Branco by Pereira Passos (1903–1905), was home to the re known as Ao Rei dos Mágicos (At the King of Magicians), where 1877 Brazil's first phone call was made. Rio was the first city outside e United States to have this technology.

Emperor Pedro II had previously visited the 1876 Philadelphia orld's Fair that celebrated the centenary of US independence. On June, he turned his attention to a Scottish inventor who wasn't at-cting much interest: Alexander Graham Bell, invited him to inspect device. Bell began to recite Shakespeare in the telephone, following ich, according to some historians, the emperor exclaimed: "My God, peaks!"

Such royal enthusiasm encouraged the rapid expansion of this sci-tific breakthrough around the country. The following year, the Ao i dos Mágicos branch of the Rodle & Chaves society was granted the ncession to install telephone lines in the city of Rio de Janeiro.

A publication of the same year, 1877, reveals that the firm also sup-ed "Indian flares", "megaphones", "lightning rods", "telegraphs" and reparations to kill rats, cockroaches and all insects", besides conjuring cks and "electric collars for children". In later logbooks, the "Casa entifica e Original" even announced its "telephones". In May 1878 e weekly *O Telephone* was launched.

The scarab is associated with Khepri, the divine manifestation of the early morning sun, and thus a symbol of the rebirth of the soul. The Egyptians frequently used it as a talisman.

There is another neo-Egyptian building at 40/42 Rua Pedro Alves, Santo Cristo (see p. 76).

BAS-RELIEFS
BY ORESTES ACQUARONE

Modernity in motion

Edifício Guinle – Avenida Rio Branco 135, corner of Rua Sete de Setembro
Metro: Carioca

In the hubbub of Avenida Rio Branco, the Guinle building (1928) one of the few major Art Deco buildings in Rio. In addition to its s guardrails with their zigzag lines, the gallery entrance hall has an ode "modernity in motion". The golden stucco painting by Orestes Acqu one (see below), above the reception desk, celebrates speed in its depicti of various means of transport: car, ship, locomotive... Although ships a locomotives were not of course new inventions, in the 20th century t began to achieve speeds that no one had previously thought possible.

1900 a car could travel at 20 km by 1930 it could reach 100 km As for aviation, in 1922 Sacadu Cabral and Gago Coutinho (b Portuguese) had made the f aerial crossing of the Atlantic fr Lisbon to Rio de Janeiro. Stre in Rio's Gamboa and Laranje neighbourhoods are named a them.

First skyscraper on Avenida Rio Branco

The Guinle building, a Gusmão, Dourado & Baldassini project was the first skyscraper on Avenida Rio Branco. It marks the begin-ning of the second generation of buildings on the former Avenid Central, the property of Eduardo Guinle. He was born after the de-molition of the building by Junnuzzi & Irmão in the early 1930s inaugurating Avenida Central.

Orestes Acquarone

Orestes Acquarone, Uruguayan designer, graphic artist and sculptor (Montevideo, 1875–1952), spent a long time in Buenos Aires be-fore settling in Rio in 1922, where he worked with some of the city's best-known publications: *Ilustração brasileira*, *O Malho* and *La Semana*. In 1926, he took up sculpture and exhibited severa times at Rio's national exhibition of fine art.

GONÇALVES DIAS MEDALLION

*Medallion commemorating the writer of the famous
Song of Exile poem*

*Rua Gonçalves Dias 40
Metro: Carioca*

A few steps from the celebrated Confeitaria Colombo café, on the right above the entrance to the Galeria dos Empregados do Comércio, is a medallion bearing the profile and name of Gonçalves Dias. The street is called after him as he lived in the house that used to stand here.

Antônio Gonçalves Dias was born in 1823 in the state of Maranhão, the son of a Portuguese merchant and a mother of mixed heritage from northern Brazil. He studied law in Portugal, where he rubbed shoulders with the great names of Portuguese literature at that time: Almeida Garrett, Alexandre Herculano and Feliciano de Castilho. At the age of 20, feeling homesick, he wrote *Canção do Exilio* (*Song of Exile*) – perhaps the best-known poem in Brazilian literature.

The palm branch and dove on the medallion evoke these lines:
My land has palm trees where the *sabiá* [native dove] sings;
The birds that sing here do not sing as they do there...
Our skies have more stars, our valleys have more flowers,
Our forests have more life. Our lives have more love.

On his return to Brazil, Gonçalves Dias carved out a brilliant career in his home town and later in Rio de Janeiro, then the capital city. He taught Latin and history, wrote for various literary journals and was patron of the 15th chair at the Brazilian Academy of Letters (see p. 50).

He also held government posts, and on his way home from an official trip to Europe in 1864 he drowned when the *Ville de Boulogne* was shipwrecked off the coast of Maranhão.

Lines from his *Song of Exile* are included in the Brazilian national anthem.

AREZZO'S STAINED-GLASS WINDOW

An Art Deco masterpiece

Rua Gonçalves Dias 13
Metro: Carioca

Almost directly across from the famous Confeitaria Colombo, the Arezzo store has occupied a charming mid-19th century house at 3 Rua Gonçalves Dias since 2012 – a street Brazilian author Machado e Assis once called "the painful road of poor husbands," renowned as the city's top shopping destination since colonial times.

The building was home to an ice-cream parlour in the late 19th century, then to Loja das Sedas (silk merchants) in the 1930s (when the fabrics were shown by models parading on a double staircase wearing the latest creations) and, between 1930 and 2010, the famous Casa Daniel (House of Daniel).

Specialising in gifts, this was for many years one of the best shops of its kind in Rio. In the early 20th century, it was very simple for future brides planning the great event: wish list at Casa Daniel, dress from Casa Canada and buffet reception at Confeitaria Colombo, all very close to each other.

When businessman Anderson Birman decided to renovate the building, which had been in a very poor state of repair for several years, he found that all Loja das Sedas' interior decor was still intact: a beautiful "Hollywood" staircase, elegant wooden furniture, but above all an Art Deco stained-glass window of exceptional quality at the head of the stairs. This large window depicting silkworms is attributed to the country's leading Art Deco graphic designer, José Carlos de Brito e Cunha, known as J. Carlos.

During the renovations, which took two years, relics from the building's previous occupants were found, such as the 19th-century Vilroy-Boch *azulejos* that can still be seen today on the ground floor – the pleasing result of some urban archaeology.

SANTA BARBARA E AS OPERARIAS
CERAMIC PANEL

From tunnel to museum

Museu National das Belas Artes (MNBA)
Avenida Rio Branco, Centro 199
(21) 2219-8474
mnba.gov.br/6_programacao/programacao.htm
Tuesday to Friday 10am–6pm, Saturdays, Sundays and public holidays,
12pm–5pm
Metro: Cinelândia

The monumental ceramic tile panel depicting St Barbara and the Workers stands in a courtyard of the National Museum of Fine Arts that is closed to the public. It can, however, be viewed from two galleries of reproductions on the first floor. This 1963 artwork by renowned Brazilian painter and engraver Djanira is a tribute to the eighteen workers killed during the construction of the Catumbi-Laranjeiras tunnel (also known as the Santa Barbara tunnel) between 1947 and 1963.

The panel was originally commissioned to decorate a chapel (now gone), built in a sort of open grotto above the tunnel roof after a rock fall during the construction work.

As access to this chapel dedicated to St Barbara, the patron saint of miners, was particularly difficult (cars can't stop in the tunnel and pedestrians are banned), the panel was hidden for almost 20 years, suffering from the effects of damp, heat and pollution.

In 1985 it was taken away for renovation, but was stored in a crate for several years before being restored and installed at the MNBA in 1996.

Amid abstract designs, this ceramic panel – one of the masterpieces of Brazilian mural art – shows the saint wrapped in a cloak, surrounded by angels and workers with their tools. Over 5,000 glazed *azulejos*, in shades ranging from dark blue to white, cover an area of more than 130 m².

At the opening of the Santa Barbara tunnel chapel, a stele was installed with an inscription in honour of the dead workers: "You who pass along this way, which our deaths have opened up through the rock, ask St Barbara that we should know life by the side of God."

Djanira, the artist who didn't want to be known as such

Born to a modest family deep in the state of São Paulo, Djanira da Motta e Silva (1914–1979) moved to Rio in the late 1930s. There she opened a lodging house in Santa Teresa that was frequented by many artists. She then began to draw regularly. An "artist" despite herself (she refused this label), she explained one day during an interview: "I didn't want to be called an 'artist'. I thought that to be an artist, I'd have to know many things that I didn't know." The MNBA holds 814 of her works (the largest surviving collection).

Liceu Literário Português azulejos

Rua Senador Dantas 118
Open office hours
Metro: Carioca

Although the neo-Manueline building of the Portuguese Literary L
ceum, just opposite the Largo da Carioca, is well known to Carioca
the lovely tiled panels in the lobby are much less so. Yet it's well wor
a visit to enjoy these scenes from Portugal's history, including the vi
tory of the first king of Portugal, Afonso Henriques, at the battle
Ourique in 1139.

The Literary Lyceum is a non-profit association founded in 1868 l
a group of Portuguese in order to spread their culture and promo
education and training. This laudable initiative is still active today.
would be good if modern Brazil were as attentive to the education
its population as the founders of the association were... The prese
building opened in 1938.

EDALLION
F EDIFÍCIO BRASILIA

hymn to Brasil

nida Rio Branco 311
ro: Cinelândia

bove the main door of the Brasilia building – a 1940s project by French architects Viret & Marmorat – a pretty medallion depicts ndigenous woman with a bow, and the Sugarloaf Mountain in the kground. The medallion is signed Humberto Cozzo (1900–1981), ading Brazilian Art Deco sculptor from São Paulo. It is a hymn to zil, its nature and its peoples, which so fascinated Europeans in the y 20th century.

Working throughout the country, Cozzo was the official sculptor of Vargas government. He also designed the bas-reliefs on the facade in the lobby of the Ministry of Finance.

The main door of the Brasilia building is the work of Raymond Sub-naster of French artistic ironwork.

MUSEU JUDAICO DO RIO DE JANEIRO

Osvaldo Aranha: a Brazilian behind the creation of Israel

Rua Mexico 90, 1st floor
(21) 2524-6451
museujudaico.org.br
Monday to Thursday 10am–4pm, Friday 10am–2pm
Metro: Cinelândia

he small and welcoming Jewish Museum, founded in 1977, aims to preserve the memory of Jewish immigration to Rio.

So a visit is an opportunity to research the subject as well as to update ir knowledge of Judaism, as the objects on display are often accomied by explanatory sheets on the cultural and historical context of ish rituals and traditions.

You'll learn about the important role played by the Brazilian Osvaldo nha (1894–1960) in the creation of the State of Israel: as President he UN General Assembly, he signed the mandate on the partition Palestine (or what was left of it, Transjordan having already been iblished in 1922 in part of ancient Palestine) at the 29 November 7 session. The mandate was directly linked to the creation of Israel 1948, which earned Aranha the eternal gratitude of Jews around the rld, although his role in the government of Getúlio Vargas was amuous: it was he who, in 1943, circulated a note around the Brazilian bassies of various European countries on the need to severely restrict number of entry visas issued to Jews. Aranha, Minister of External ations at the time, even rather abruptly dismissed the Brazilian conin Marseille, Luiz Martins de Souza Dantas, who had authorised s for Jews.

The museum also has a collection of menorah and chanukiah that nonstrates the difference between the two. The menorah is a candeum with seven branches, as originally made by Moses: it symbolises burning bush he witnessed on Mount Sinai. It became one of the facts of the Tabernacle, then of the Temple of Jerusalem, and is one he symbols of Judaism.

The chanukiah is a candelabrum with nine branches (eight plus) used by Jews during the celebration of nukkah, the festival of light: this commorates the liberation of the Temple of isalem following the Maccabean revolt inst the Seleucids.

According to tradition, the victorious eans found only a small flask of pure oloil to kindle the Temple menorah. This which would normally have burned for y one day, miraculously lasted for eight s.

PORTINARI PANELS AT PALÁCIO GUSTAVO CAPANEMA

Little-known Carioca masterpieces

Rua da Imprensa 16, Castelo – Metro Cinelândia
(21) 2220-1490
Monday to Friday 10am–6pm (admission free)

Although Capanema Palace is an icon of modern architecture, second floor is home to unknown works on Carioca themes commissioned for the building) by modernist painter Cândido Po nari (1903–1962).

At the elevator exit is the *Jogos infantis* (Children's Games) exh tion, a tribute to the huge mural of the same name that dominates space and shows typical childhood activities from the Brazilian inter

Admire the tubular steel sofas, probably by Lúcio Costa, and O Niemeyer's vast carpet. And have a look through the windows to disco the external architecture – a powerful example of Brazilian modernism

Just next door is the Portinari room, with a series of the artist's pai ings that form a large mural depicting the cycles of the country's ec omy: *pau-brasil*, sugar cane, cattle, ore prospecting, cotton, tea, cof cocoa, iron, palm and rubber.

In the Gilberto Freyre conference room on the lower floor, two pa-
s evoke the early days of education under the Jesuits. This set of fres-
d panels is typical of Portinari's work, highlighting his awareness of
ial issues.

On the second floor, paintings from the abstract series *Os quatro
nentos* (The Four Elements) can be seen. As these are offices, access is
ited, but with a little luck you can catch a glimpse of them... *Ar* (Air)
n the former office of Minister Gustavo Capanema (1900–1985),
le *Água* (Water) is in the office of his principal private secretary, poet
·los Drummond de Andrade (1902–1987). The other two elements,
o (Fire) and *Terra* (Earth), are in adjacent rooms.

At street level, Portinari's *azulejos* decorate the exterior of the buil-
ling – they all feature marine motifs. Specialist Carlos Zílio claims
his work is not only "the most important by the artist, but also one
f the most expressive of modernism". There's a story attached to their
reation. When Capanema discovered the marine panels decorated
vith fish, he considered the result "aesthetically unsatisfactory". This
emark is said to have been elicited by the prominent facial features of
oth minister and fish. Portinari made some replacement tiles, which
vould explain the starfish that appear on one of the panels.

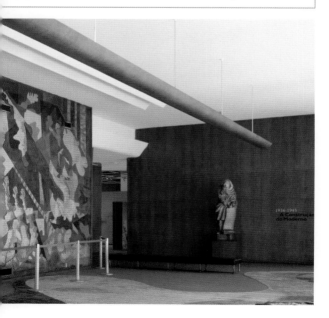

CAPANEMA HANGING GARDENS

A roof garden hidden from view

Palácio Gustavo Capanema
Rua da Imprensa 16, Castelo
Monday to Friday 10am–6pm (admission free)
(21) 2220-1490
Metro: Cinelândia

On the second floor of Capanema Palace, a roof garden (which c
be seen from the street) is an example of the principles
modernism as set out by Swiss architect Le Corbusier (1887–1965).
underrated garden with its sinuous lines, designed by landscape archi
Roberto Burle Marx (1909–1994), only features Brazilian plant spec

ong them stands the red granite *Mulher sentada* (Seated Woman) stat-
, the work of Adriana Janacópulos (1897–1978). The garden is similar
another at street level, also by Burle Marx, with lines mimicking waves
eracting with Portinari's marine-inspired *azulejo* panels (see p. 47).
ere's also a roof garden on the 16th floor, with limited access, which
addition to offering a fine view lets you appreciate the "conversation"
ween the hanging garden and its counterpart outside.

A sophisticated statue

Modernist sculptor Celso Antônio (1896–1984) created the
Maternidade (Maternity) statue that stood at the head of the palace's
lovely spiral staircase until 1952, before disappearing and then reap-
pearing some months later. We now know that Lúcio Costa, then
working for the Heritage Department, had asked for the statue to
be removed because he considered it unsuitable for the site. It was
offered to the town hall and installed in a garden at Praia de Botafogo
near the Church of the Immaculate Conception, where it still can
be seen today.

The minister who wanted a modern building

The palace, built between 1936 and 1945 as the seat of the Ministry
of Education and Health (MES) – now the Ministry of Education
and Culture (MEC) – is listed as national heritage. It is known lo-
cally as the "MEC building" despite being named after the minister
responsible, Gustavo Capanema.

The project provoked heated debate. Despite receiving 34 tenders,
Capanema (who wanted a modern building) caused controversy by
ignoring the result and separately commissioning Lúcio Costa, one
of the modern architects excluded from the tender.

Other architects incorporated into Costa's team included Oscar
Niemeyer, Jorge Moreira, Afonso Reidy, Carlos Leão and Ernani
Vasconcelos, who followed the modernist principles of Le
Corbusier.

Other than the roof garden, modernist features include the rows of
10 m high pillars that create an open public space below; the glass
facade opposite the protective sun canopy; granite blind gables; the
spiral staircase leading to the upper floor; and modern sculptures.

GUIDED TOUR OF ACADEMIA BRASILEIRA DE LETRAS

A great time was had by all

Avenida Presidente Wilson 203
Guided tour every Wednesday, 2pm–3pm (minimum age: 12)
Réservations required: visita.guiada@academia.org.br or (21) 3974-2500
Admission free
Metro: Cinelândia

E very Wednesday, you can visit the charming interiors of the B
zilian Academy of Letters. The tour is led by professional act
who recount the history of the academy and from time to time re

nous passages from Brazilian literature, such as the Gonçalves Dias
ng of Exile (see p. 37).

The visit may seem a bit kitsch at first (the actors are in late 19th-cen-
y costume), but you have a great time: the actors are very good,
metimes funny, as the representatives of the Academy who welcome
itors, and you learn something too.

Note that there are Rio school students on almost all the tours, so
od humour and a little horseplay are to be expected.

A vestige of the Exposition of 1922

The building is one of the few vestiges of the Independence
Centenary International Exposition of 1922 (see following double-
page spread). Built in 1922 as the French pavilion, it is a copy
of the Petit Trianon at Versailles (see photo). The building was
presented to the Brazilian Academy of Letters by France in 1923,
along with some of its fittings. The small garden at the back was
designed by Burle Marx.

Also part of the Academy, the Palácio Austregésilo de Athayde (named after an academician), next door, was built in 1979 on the
site of the former British pavilion at the 1922 Expo. Reservations
are theoretically required but can be made for five minutes later...
You can visit the second-floor area devoted to Machado de Assis
one of the greatest Brazilian authors of all time), with memorabilia
and furniture from the writer's last home. The first-floor Centro
de Memória (Centre of Memories) has a collection of historical
photographs relating to the Academy.
Open Monday to Friday 9am–6pm

Exposição internacional do Centenário do Brasil (1922–1923)

The Independence Centenary International Exposition was the first World's Fair to be held after the 1914–1918 war.

More than 20 pavilions were built, as well as two monumental gateways and an amusement park. Initially designed to be a national Expo, like that of 1908 which was also held in Rio (see p. 188), it benefited from the participation of fourteen countries.

More than 6,000 national and international exhibitors were represented. The Brazilian section of the exposition stretched from Praça XV to the former fort at Calabouço (Calaboose Point, now the National Historical Museum).

The pavilions were built along what was then called Avenida das Nações (now Avenida Presidente Wilson).

An estimated 3 million visitors attended, 200,000 of them on opening day.

The exposition transformed the urban space and encouraged the use of new techniques and building materials. Ironically, this event celebrating the end of the colonial period also sanctioned neocolonialism as a national style.

The celebrations were marked by the opening speech of President Epitácio Pessoa (1865–1942) – the country's first radio broadcast. A special lighting system had been installed for nocturnal visits and, in another first for a World's Fair, films were screened.

Many of the pavilions were built on recent landfill from the levelling of Morro do Castelo (see p. 59) for the Expo site.

Exposição do Centenario - 1922

Other reminders of the 1922–1923 Expo

In addition to the Petit Trianon (see p. 51), two other buildings were built for the International Exposition commemorating the centenary of Brazil's independence, held from September 1922 to July 1923. Now the Museu da Imagem et do Som (MIS – Museum of Image and Sound) and the Centro Cultural do Ministério da Saúde (CCMS – Cultural Centre of the Ministry of Health), both in Praça Marechal Âncora, the buildings were then used as the Federal District Pavilion and Statistics Pavilion respectively.

A group of three former military buildings renovated to accommodate the Industries Pavilion are now home to the Museu Histórico Nacional (MHN – National Historical Museum). The United States Consulate (147 Avenida Presidente Wilson) stands on the site where the North American Pavilion was built.

The Pavilhão Carlos Lopes, where Portuguese industrial products were exhibited, was relocated to Lisbon in 1932. (See *Secret Lisbon* in this series of guidebooks.)

SANTA LUZIA CAR-PARK WALL

A historic wall recovered

In front of Rua Santa Luzia 255
24/7
Metro: Cinelândia

Anyone who uses the Santa Luzia underground car park will alrea
know about this. But passers-by strolling along the sidewalks v
never guess that the remains of a historic wall can be seen down ther

There was a time when the waves almost lapped against the near
church of Santa Luzia. There was even a beach of that name. Since the
the chunks of land successively reclaimed from the sea have gradua
filled the space between church and ocean.

The first embankment was built under the administration of Pere
Passos, in the early 20th century, to make way for Avenida Beira M
To contain the boulevard and protect it from the force of the waves, t

efecture built a retaining wall that followed the shoreline from Santa
sa da Misericórdia in the direction of Glória.

With the razing of Morro do Castelo to construct the embankment
ere the 1922 Independence Centenary International Exposition was
ged (see preceding page), this wall has disappeared, and is now buried
d forgotten.

However, in the 2000s the prefecture authorised the construction
several underground car parks, one below the under-used lanes of
enida Presidente Antônio Carlos.

When the workers started digging, they were faced with a huge obs-
le. Once the wall had been identified, a thorny issue remained: how
preserve this archaeological find while allowing the parking lot to
ahead? The solution was to open a breach in the wall wide enough
vehicles and to preserve the two side sections, the last witnesses to a
ntentious maritime project that had left little trace.

In order to pour the concrete needed to surface the car park, two large
tions of the wall had to be lifted to the surface and then reinstalled once
floor had been laid, using two massive cranes.

The wall turned out to be so well built that the mortar in the joints
dn't even crack, meaning that the sections could be raised and lowered
one piece.

Go down into the car park today, via the stairs or the elevator, and you
still see them on the nearest part of the church.

For more about the land Rio has reclaimed from the sea, see the
following double-page spread.

Rio: a city built on land largely reclaimed from the sea

The Rio landscape has changed enormously since the arrival of the first settlers: to enlarge the city, and sometimes for health reasons, beaches, ponds, swamps and even rivers were filled in. Hills were levelled, and the city created new vistas.

In the early 18th century, Lagoa de Santo Antônio (Saint Anthony's Lagoon), which joined the sea at high tide, was filled in and became what is now Largo da Carioca. The site of Rua dos Arcos used to be Lagoa do Desterro, drained in 1643. Lagoa do Boqueirão da Ajuda, for its part, was filled in with earth from the nearby hill, Morro das Mangueiras, to build the Passeio Público (Public Promenade, see p. 112). A little further south, at the level of the current Largo do Machado, Lagoa da Carioca and the Catete river (see p. 128) were also filled in.

A huge flooded mangrove swamp used to border Saco de São Cristóvão, a long stretch of seashore from the current Praça XI to the level of the Novo Rio bus station and Santo Cristo neighbourhood (where Praia Formosa and Saco do Alferes were located until the early 20th century). This area started to be reclaimed during the colonial period: the aim was to clean up the sites and facilitate movement between Palácio de São Cristóvão and Paço Real (nowadays known as Paço Imperial) on Praça XV. As the area to be filled in was considerable and the work costly, only a narrow route was made for the carriages of the imperial court. The drainage ditch running along the so-called Caminho do Aterrado (Terraced Path) was converted into a canal (Canal do Mangue) in the 16th century. In the early 20th century, during the construction of the new port of Rio, the canal was extended as far as the shore.

In a bid to modernise the city and mark the beginning of the Republic, the 20th century began under the sign of great urban projects. In the centre, the beaches of Dom Manuel and Peixe (now Praça XV) disappeared. Prainha (a small beach), on the site of what is now Praça Mauá, along with Saúde and Gamboa beaches, were covered by the foundations of the new port.

The earth used for this landfill came from Morro do Senado, the hill having made way for Praça da Cruz Vermelha.

In 1922, with the levelling of Morro do Castelo (see p. 59), the beaches of Santa Luzia (Castelo), Ajuda (Cinelândia), Glória, Russel and Boqueirão (opposite the Passeio Público, see p. 112) as far as Calabouço (near the National Historical Museum) were filled in. This land reclaimed from the sea joined that of Avenida

Beira-Mar (opened in 1906) and ran from the Obelisk to the end of the present Avenida Rio Branco, as far as Botafogo.
In the early 1950s, Aterro do Flamengo (reclaimed from the sea) was constructed thanks to the partial destruction of Morro de Santo Antônio.
In the place where the hill used to rise, there are new avenues with large buildings and the Cathedral of St Sebastian.
Part of Copacabana beach, in the Zona Sul, was built over in the 1970s in order to extend Avenida Atlantica. As for Lagoa Rodrigues de Freitas, over the years it has lost almost 40 per cent of its surface to sports clubs and residential buildings (built legally or illegally).
This urban policy hasn't been restricted to downtown Rio and the Zona Sul. In the Zona Norte, for example, the area from Point do Caju to Praia de Maria Angu is now covered with the *favelas* of Maré neighbourhood (see p. 306) and part of Avenida Brasil and Linha Vermelha. The archipelago that used to jut out near Enseada de Inhaúma has been integrated with Fundão island, home to the Universidade Federal do Rio de Janeiro campus.

CENTRO DA CIDADE DO RIO DE JANEIRO
VARIAÇÃO FÍSICA DA ORLA MARÍTIMA
EDUARDO CANABRAVA BARREIROS
1965

CONVENÇÕES
Área primitiva
Área
conquistada ao mar

ART DECO DETAILS OF THE TRIBUNAL REGIONAL DO TRABALHO

One of the city's most outstanding Art Deco buildings

Avenida Presidente Antônio Carlos 105
Metro: Carioca

he former Ministry of Labour, now the Regional Labour Court, is one of Rio's most striking buildings with its futuristic, sleek, w-York-skyscraper style and high-quality Art Deco ironwork.

The building, designed in 1936 by architect Mario Santos Maia (in laboration with Affonso Eduardo Reidy, responsible for the Museu Arte Moderna in the 1950s), features doors, gates and wroughtiron ndows made in the workshops of Pellegrino and Fernandes, master nworkers.

The interior aesthetic evokes the Bauhaus style, dominated by eco-mical, austere solutions: the stairways and handrails are of chrome el and the walls are glass brick, giving a truly streamlined look.

The razing of Morro do Castelo to make way for Esplanada Castelo and one of Rio's centres of Art Deco

After Morro do Castelo (Castle hill) was demolished in the 1920s, the question arose of what to do with the site, which came to be known as Esplanada Castelo (Castle Esplanade).

Although it lay empty for some years, part of it was used by the 1922 exposition commemorating the centenary of Brazil's inde-pendence (see p. 52).

Once the pavilions had been dismantled (with a few exceptions, such as the French pavilion – see p. 51), doubts persisted: what to do with this huge area in the centre of Rio?

On taking power in 1930, Getúlio Vargas, the "permanent pre-sident" (a euphemism used by North Americans to refer to the dictator), soon found a new use for the site, imagining it as a fe-deral capital.

Hence the city's largest concentration of Art Deco buildings: the ministries, courts and administrations of all sectors were housed in new, modern buildings, indicative of the global power that Brazil had become.

A "New Brazil" exhibition was even inaugurated in 1938, show-casing models of completed buildings and others that were still at the planning stage.

CERAMICS AT THE MINISTÉRIO DA FAZENDA

Works of art on the top floor of a ministry building

Museu da Fazenda Federal
Avenida Presidente Antônio Carlos 375
Guided tours (Portuguese only), Monday to Friday 9am–4pm
To book, call (21) 3805-2003 / 3805-2004
Admission free
Metro: Cinelândia

Very few Cariocas know that the terrace of the Ministry of Finance, on the 14th floor, hides a real gem of Brazilian modern art: pan- by artist and muralist Paulo Werneck (1907–1987) that incorporate amic mosaics.

Luiz Moura, the architect responsible for implementing the Minis- of Finance project, actually preferred more conservative designs. He rprised everyone by commissioning Werneck for these five ceramic nels inspired by indigenous culture and tropical nature: "You're part the modern trend but you can draw," he said. "You're going to design e ministry's mosaics. The theme is up to you."

Werneck, widely considered to be Brazil's greatest 20th-century mo- c maker, was the first to work from live models. Years later, he de- ibed part of his work in these words: "The Indian man was based on rave in the service of the Jesuits who defended their missions; he was led Sepé Tiaraju. The Indian woman, I don't remember. One of the nels depicts the Amazon, we see a toucan. On another, we have wild cks, a lot of water, palm trees…"

This was the first time that Werneck had worked in ceramics, thanks the cooperation of Jorge Ludolf, regarded as the country's largest ce- nics manufacturer at the time.

The factory produced a wide variety of colours, "with totally stable aterials and colours that are no longer made", Werneck claimed.

A viewpoint that throws light on Morro do Castelo

The terrace doesn't only have a wonderful view, it's one of the best places to appreciate the site of the historic Morro do Castelo (see p. 59). This was levelled to make way for the present esplanade and the Ministries of Finance, Labour, Education and Health, among other buildings. The earth excavated from the hill was used to re-claim land from the sea, including the former beach in front of the Igrega de Santa Luzia, the church on the seashore where part of the Independence Centenary International Exposition was held in 1922 (see p. 52).

The terrace also features two glazed ceramic sculptures, again on an indigenous theme, by the artist Leão Velloso (1899–1966). The Ministry of Finance also boasts a magnificent interior staircase (see following double-page spread).

STAIRWAY OF THE FORMER MINISTRY OF FINANCE

A spectacular and little-known flight of stairs

Palácio da Fazenda
Avenida Presidente Antônio Carlos 375
Guided tours (in Portuguese) Monday to Friday, 9am–4pm (reservations
by phone at (21) 3805-2003 / 3805-2004)
Admission free
Metro: Cinelândia

As you enter the elevator lobby of Palácio da Fazenda (former Ministry of Finance), you'll immediately notice an imposing double ght of stairs. Two large chandeliers seem to float over the wide stairlls, of extreme lightness of touch despite their marble steps and gilded tal guardrails. From the first floor, the two flights meet and form just e spectacular spiral staircase, as you'll see during the guided tour. The lings are the work of Oreste Fabbro, who also designed the entrance ors and the decorative grilles at the counters.

The building, inaugurated in 1943, was the Ministry of Finance headquarters until Brasilia became the capital city in the early 1960s. Construction work began amid some controversy. The modernist project proposed by Wladimir Alves de Souza and Eneas Silva, winners of the architectural tender, was dismissed by the Minister of Finance, Arthur de Souza Costa (1893–1957), who preferred a neo-classical style. Such was his influence that he presented the project team with a photo of an Italian neoclassical building, declaring (even though plans for the new building were ready): "This is how I want the facade to look."

As part of the modernisation of Rio de Janeiro undertaken by the Getúlio Vargas government (see p. 120), two buildings were completed around the same time in hugely different styles: the neoclassical Palácio da Fazenda and the Ministry of Education and Health (Capanema – see p. 49), one of the main symbols of Brazilian modernism.

Palácio da Fazenda also features pretty modernist ceramics on the 14th floor (see following double-page spread).

Originally, the Ministry of Finance was to be built on Avenida Passos, near Praça Tiradentes, hence the demolition of the Imperial Academy of Fine Arts, designed by French architect Grandjean de Montigny and inaugurated in 1826. Only its entrance portico has been preserved: it is now at the Botanical Garden (see p. 202). On the site of the building, an infinitely sad car park struggles to forget its predecessor in the heart of the city.

IGREJA DE NOSSA SENHORA DO BONSUCESSO

Memories of a prolonged miracle

Rua Santa Luzia 206
Tuesday to Thursday 8am–5pm, Friday and Saturday 8am–12pm
Metro: Cinelândia

A n antique table in the sacristy of the church of Our Lady of Good
Success (the entrance is on Rua Santa Luzia – the main doorway is
most always closed) recalls a miracle that lasted an hour and a half and
s lingered in people's memories for almost four centuries.

In 1637, Father Miguel Costa arrived in town with the first image of
om Successo", the original saint worshipped in Brazil, and obtained
rmission to install it on the altar at the Igreja da Misericórdia (Church
Mercy).

The saint's feast day was always on the first Sunday after 8 Septem-
r. The miracle took place at the first celebration: "*In the year 1639, on
September, during the Sunday in the octave of the nativity of the saint,
 day when the first feast of Our Lady of Good Success was celebrated, at
 introduction of the Holy Sacrament, the Virgin appeared in the form in
 ich she is painted; she was seen by three priests over a period of an hour
 d a half and this miracle has been recognised.*"

For an hour and a half, each worshipper taking communion actually
 v the image of the Virgin, as explained by the text and the icon, which
 u can still see today.

According to Brother Miguel de São Francisco, the miracle was
 eated shortly afterwards when a novena (prayers repeated for nine
 nsecutive days) was celebrated to alleviate the drought that was dev-
 ating the city.

The saint's popularity grew to the point where she was considered
 tron of the Santa Casa hospital.

EARBY

ie eyes of the clock

 the same sacristy, almost directly
 posite the image of the miraculous
 rgin, a remarkable clock often
 es unnoticed.

 t stop a moment to look closely
 it and you'll realise that the eyes
 the chubby, friendly face inside,
 ove the dial itself, accompany the
 ing of the pendulum.

 glance to the right, a glance to the
 t, as if this character was watching
  passage of time...

ESTAÇÃO DE HIDROAVIÕES STAIRCASE

The Seaplane Station is still at Santos Dumont Airport

Instituto Histórico-Cultural da Aeronáutica (INCAER)
Praça Marechal Âncora 15-A (next to Club da Aeronáutica)
(21) 2101-4966 / 2101-4967
incaer.aer.mil.br
Monday to Friday 8.30am–12pm (call to confirm summer schedule)
Admission free
Metro: Cinelândia

Although no longer operating, the Seaplane Station at Santos Dumont Airport, one of the icons of Brazilian modernist architecture, ll exists. Its most interesting feature is probably the elegant concrete ral staircase, rising 5.4 m between ground and first floor.

The building, with its spare and simple lines, has free-standing fa-des with a large expanse of glass that originally allowed a clear view of city on one side and Guanabara bay on the other. Le Corbusier's five ints of modern architecture feature in this project: supporting walls placed by reinforced concrete columns (pilotis); free design of ground n; free facade (separated from structural function); horizontal ribbon ndows; and terrace or roof garden encouraging integration with the dscape.

The building, listed as historic and artistic national heritage in 1957, s suffered over time. The windows are now coated with a dark film cut the glare of the tropical sun and reduce the heat inside. By the ne token, the great hall on the ground floor – the former departure nge – has been converted into a conference room. The first floor, ich used to be a pleasant waiting area with overstuffed chairs, res-rant and bar, has become a storage space, although the outstanding minium-coated bar counter is still there.

Also on the first floor, a terrace offers a fine view of Ilha Fiscal (Fiscal and in Guanabara Bay, where the border guards used to operate). om here you can also glimpse the original little spiral staircase leading the garden and the covered walkway for boarding the seaplanes, now t of the Aerospace Club (private).

The Seaplane Station, opened in 1938, was designed by architect tilio Corrêa Lima, winner of the previous year's architectural tenders. aviation technology advanced, the station closed in 1942 and was nporarily ceded to the Aeronautical Club. Since 1986 INCAER has ken over the building. Corrêa Lima was killed nearby in 1943 when plane crash-landed at Santos Dumont Airport.

The INCAER library has some 8,000 Brazilian and foreign aero-nautical books, some of them rare or early editions.

OVAL PANELS
BY LEANDRO JOAQUIM

The only known painting of whaling in Guanabara Bay

Museu Histórico Nacional
Praça Marechal Âncora (next to Praça XV)
(21) 3299-0300 / 3299-0324
museuhistoriconacional.com.br
Wednesday to Sunday, 10am–5pm
Free on Sundays
Metro: Cinelândia, then about twenty minutes' walk

he oval panels by Brazilian artist Leandro Joaquim (dating from
around 1738–1798), on show at the National Historical Museum,
a rare depiction of 18th-century Rio and Guanabara Bay. They are a
ual chronicle of various aspects of daily life, different types of people
d architectural details of the time. The works also illustrate the im-
rtance of the sea to the city – four of them are seascapes and the other
o landscapes are set by the sea.

The pictures are: *Vista da Igrega da Glória* (View from the Church
Glória), with the church that stands there today on the beach, since
dfilled (see p. 123), and fishermen hauling a net; *Vista da Lagoa do
queirão e dos Arcos da Carioca* (View from the Lagoon of Boqueirão
d the Arches of Carioca), which shows the Lapa Arches and Cariocas
ing about their business before the lagoon was filled in to form the
sseio Público (see p. 112), and in the foreground, a wave breaking on
e beach; *Procissão ou romarío maritima ao Hospital dos Lázaros* (Proces-
n or Maritime Pilgrimage to the Leprosarium), showing the hospital
at still exists and a procession of boats at the beach of São Cristóvão,
ckfilled long ago; *Revista militar no Largo do Paço* (Military Review in
e Largo do Paco), which proves that what is now Praça XV has many
th-century elements – Paço Imperial (Imperial Palace), then the vice-
's residence, the churches of Carmo (Carmel) and the Third Order of
rmelites, the Arch of Teles and, on what was the dockside, the Foun-
n of Mestre Valentim; *Cena marítima* (Maritime Scene), showing a
iting British squadron anchored alongside Villegagnon fortress, now
e Naval Academy; and finally, *Pesca da baleia na Baía de Guanabara*
/haling in the Bay of Guanabara), the only known painting of every-
y fishing in the bay during the 18th century.

The panels (eight originally, but two have been lost) were commis-
ned to decorate the pavilions of the Passeio Público terraces, and are
ong the country's first sea and landscape paintings by a Brazilian
ist.

SUGAR LOAVES AT THE NATIONAL HISTORICAL MUSEUM

An example of how the famous Sugar Loaf got its name

Museu Histórico Nacional
Praça Marechal Âncora (next to Praça XV)
(21) 3299-0300 / 3299-0324
museuhistoriconacional.com.br
Wednesday to Sunday, 10am–5pm
Free on Sundays
Metro: Cinelândia, then about 20 minutes' walk

or those who have never really understood the origin of the name "Sugar Loaf", Rio's National Historical Museum has had the brilliant idea of including two real sugar loaves in its collection.

As found in the museum, a sugar loaf is a conical block of sugar (the same shape as Urca's famous Sugarloaf Mountain and the cones used for refining sugar).

This is the form in which loaf sugar was sold until the late 19th century, when it was gradually replaced by granulated or cube sugar, although loaf is still used in some traditional societies.

The great advantage of the loaf shape is that it keeps really well: it resists the ravages of time, unlike other forms of packaging such as those used for granulated or cubed sugar. Loaf sugar can be transported over long distances with little risk of damage, hence its success in remote, inaccessible and impoverished regions where price is all-important.

The technical processes of sugar manufacturing have determined its conical shape: the loaf mould, made from earthenware, metal or wood, consisted of a relatively wide base rising in a conical shape with a hole at the end.

The inverted mould (hole at the bottom) was filled with sugar-cane juice and the top covered with a layer of clay.

Every day, for 30 to 40 days, water was poured into the mould through the sugarcane juice, to drain out of the hole at the bottom.

At the end of this filtration process, the whitest, most refined sugar was at the top of the loaf, the darkest at the bottom.

LIBRARY OF THE MUSEU HISTÓRICO NACIONAL

A forgotten library

Praça Marechal Âncora (near Praça XV)
(21) 3299-0351
mhn.biblioteca@museus.gov.br – museuhistoriconacional.com.br
Monday to Friday 2pm–5pm
Metro: Cinelândia, then about 20 minutes' walk

Few visitors to the National Historical Museum realise that it so has a library. There is a good reason for this: in order to fin it, visitors have to go through the main entrance and up to the fi floor, and, instead of visiting the first room on the right, take the do leading to the museum's small terrace. This leads to the library whic in addition to its book collections (all available for consultation), h beautiful painted ceilings by Carlos Oswald (1882–1971), who al decorated the Large Industries Pavilion at the 1922 International F position. The library now occupies part of the original pavilion buil ing (see p. 53).

AS-RELIEFS AT
HE CENTRO ADMINISTRATIVO
O TRIBUNAL DE JUSTIÇA

t Deco in Praça XV

ça XV de Novembre 2

esigned in 1941 by architect Humberto Nabuco dos Santos, the
Administrative Centre of the Court of Justice, in Praça XV, fea-
es some remarkable Art Deco bas-reliefs whose existence is unknown
many Cariocas.

The sculptures by Armando Sócrates Schnoor, set on top of two
shaped columns at the entrance to the building, depict men from
azil's different ethnic groups engaged in fishing.

The building previously housed the federal fishing warehouse and
Companhia Nacional de Abastecimento (CONAB), the National
pply Company.

Lapa – Centro – Gamboa – Saúde

1. RARE NEO-EGYPTIAN BUILDING — 76
2. OBSERVATÓRIO DO VALONGO — 78
3. ITAMARATY HISTORICAL AND DIPLOMATIC MUSEUM — 80
4. PALÁCIO EPISCOPAL AND FORTALEZA DA CONCEIÇÃO — 82
5. DI CAVALCANTI FRESCOES ON THE NEWSROOM — 86
6. STATUE OF SÃO DISMAS — 88
7. LAGARTO FOUNTAIN ON RUA FREI CANECA — 90
8. MUSEU DA POLÍCIA MILITAR DO ESTADO DO RIO DE JANEIRO — 91
9. FACADE OF THE FORMER LAMBERT PERFUME AND SOAP FACTORY — 92
10. MUSEU DA POLÍCIA CIVIL WAXWORKS — 94
11. RIGHT ARM OF NOSSA SENHORA DOS PRAZERES' STATUE — 95
12. RAISED FLOOR OF IGREJA DO SANTÍSSIMO SACRAMENTO DA ANTIGA SÉ — 96
13. CASA FRANKLIN FACADE — 98
14. MUSEU DA BÍBLIA — 99
15. DI CAVALCANTI PANELS AT THE JOÃO CAETANO THEATRE — 100
16. STATUE OF JOÃO CAETANO — 102
17. GOLDEN ROSE OF THE MUSEU ARQUIDIOCESANO DE ARTE SACRA — 106
18. *AZULEJOS* AT THE CLUBE DOS DEMOCRÁTICOS — 108
19. ESCOLA DE MÚSICA CONCERT HALL — 110
20. INVERNO STATUE IN THE PASSEIO PÚBLICO — 112
21. SECRETS OF THE INSTITUTO HISTÓRICO E GEOGRÁFICO BRASILEIRO — 114

RARE NEO-EGYPTIAN BUILDING

Egyptian allegories

Rua Pedro Alves 40 / 42
Taxi recommended

n the Santo Cristo neighbourhood, not far from the remarkable Fábrica Bhering (former chocolate factory at 28 Rua Orested – not to be
issed), the neo-Egyptian building at 40 / 42 Rua Pedro Alves stands
t amid the warehouses and other commercial or industrial buildings.

The 1910 construction is one of the city's most stunningly beautiful
chitectural achievements, and still in perfect condition.

The variety of its decoration is particularly striking, with original ver-
ons of symbols such as palm-shaped capitals, the rising Sun (allegory
the god Ra), falcon wings (allegory of the god Horus) and winged
arabs (symbol of the rebirth of the soul).

There is another neo-Egyptian building in downtown Rio (see
p. 34).

Although the worldwide fashion for Egyptian-style buildings developed after Napoleon Bonaparte's Egyptian campaign of 1798, he
actually only followed a trend already well established in Europe.
From the mid-18th century, young artists went to Italy to seek the
Etruscan and Egyptian origins of Roman art. At the time of the
French Revolution, which was heavily influenced by Freemasonry,
there already was a lively interest in the cult of the dead and the
mysteries of Egyptian art dear to the Freemasons.

OBSERVATÓRIO DO VALONGO

*Observe the stars, Sun and Moon from
the city centre*

Ladeira Pedro Antônio 43
(21) 2263-0685 – ov@astro.ufrj.br – ov.ufrj.br
Visits: 1pm–4pm every working day by reservation at extensao@ov.ufrj.br,
including a tour of the campus
In June, July and August, observation on Wednesday, 6pm–9.30pm, weather
permitting
Admission free

Valongo Observatory, the astronomical observatory of the UFR
is less well known than Brazil's National Observatory at São Cr.
tóvão. On the heights of Morro da Conceição, it's easily accessible d
rectly from Ladeira do Pedro Antônio, overlooking Rua da Conceiçã
Twice a month the observatory invites the public along to observe th
stars.

After a half-hour presentation on an astronomical topic (during our ⸱it the topic was "stellar winds – source of the *Aurora Borealis*"), you ⸱ove straight to the telescopes (there's usually one set up on the lawn in ⸱nt of the main building).

The atmosphere is relaxed, far from the crowds that frequent São ⸱istóvão. Depending on the timing of your visit, you'll see Mercury, ⸱turn and its rings and, of course, the truly unmissable Moon – on ⸱od days you can even make out the contours of the craters on its ⸱rface. The experience is totally unmissable.

In addition to the outdoor telescope, the Coudé telescope under its ⸱etty wooden dome lets you observe Saturn in detail. Although you ⸱ay get a better picture of the planet online, seeing it 'for real' through ⸱e telescope is something special.

On weekdays you can visit the observatory itself, whose main attrac-⸱n is the Cooke & Sons telescope under a beautiful antique dome in ⸱e main building.

Valongo Observatory owes its existence to Manoel Pereira Re-⸱ (1837–1922). He fell out with Emmanuel Liais (1826–1900), the ⸱ench director of the Observatório Imperial, where Pereira Reis worked ⸱ an astronomer. In association with Joaquim Galdino Pimentel and ⸱dré Gustavo Paulo de Frontin, he acquired land on Morro de Santo ⸱tônio, near the Escola Politécnica, where they built and gradually ⸱veloped a small observatory.

The destruction of Morro de Santo Antônio (see following dou-⸱e-page spread) and Morro do Castelo (then home to the Imperial Ob-⸱rvatory) in the 1920s was an incentive to transfer the observatory to ⸱ present location between 1924 and 1926.

The main entrance and the buildings that house the domes for the ⸱ooke and Pazos telescopes were reconstructed in an almost identical ⸱le to the Santo Antônio buildings.

© Observatorio do Valongo

ITAMARATY HISTORICAL AND DIPLOMATIC MUSEUM

A forgotten jewel

Avenida Marechal Floriano 196
Visits by appointment only
(21) 2253-2828
ererio.museu@itamaraty.gov.br
To visit the library Monday to Friday, 10am–5pm, phone (21) 2253-5720

By appointment only (see above), it is possible to visit the Historic and Diplomatic Museum in the Itamaraty Palace, headquarters of the Ministry of Foreign Affairs between 1899 and 1970.

In addition to the collections (paintings, furniture, decorations and objects associated with the history of Brazilian diplomacy), visitors can see the remarkable rooms that now house the museum: the Indian salon with its magnificent indigenous-style wallpaper (unfortunately in bad condition) as well as the ballroom and the former office of the Baron of Rio Branco, Minister of Foreign Affairs between 1902 and 1912. He played a crucial role in Brazilian political life.

It was his diplomatic skill in particular that resolved the border disputes with Argentina, France (the frontier with French Guiana) and, most notably, Bolivia. In 1903, he negotiated the transfer of the state of Acre from Bolivia to Brazil. Rio Branco, the state capital, was named after him.

Visitors can go out onto a terrace with a lovely view over the historic library, ornamental lake and stately palm trees located within the inner garden. The palace owes its existence to Francisco José da Rocha (1806–1883), Count of Itamaraty, a wealthy trader in coffee and precious stones. He commissioned José Maria Jacinto Rebelo, a disciple of Grandjean de Montigny, to build the palace in 1854.

In 1889, the house was sold to the Republic of Brazil, which made it the headquarters of the presidency before it was used as the Ministry of Foreign Affairs.

The historic library

After the creation of Avenida Presidente Vargas, a decision was taken to construct a new building for the library. It was designed between 1927 and 1930 by the Scottish architect Robert Prentice (also responsible for the Leopoldina railway station, see p. 279) and his Austrian colleague Anton Floderer (who designed the Lacerda Elevator, in Salvador de Bahia). No expense was spared: the windows and bronze doors came from England, the artificial ventilation and a paper disinfection machine were imported from Germany, while the linoleum flooring and a machine for refrigerating drinking water came from the United States. Please note: entrance to the museum does not include access to the library. A separate reservation is required (see above).

PALÁCIO EPISCOPAL AND FORTALEZA DA CONCEIÇÃO

A historical look at the city

Rua Major Daemon 81
(21) 2223-2177 for reservations
5dl.eb.mil.br
Monday to Thursday, 8am–4pm, Friday 8am–12pm

he 5ª Divisão de Levantamento (5th Division of Topographic Surveys) has been installed since 1922 in unique premises in the rt of Morro da Conceição. Despite its central location, many Car-as remain unfamiliar with this particular hill. The buildings, listed 1938, include the beautiful old Bishop's Palace with its charming ister (built in 1702), and the former Fortress of the Immaculate nception, established in 1713 as part of the city's defence system.

You can book a tour round the Museu Cartográfico do Serviço Ge-ráfico do Exército (Army Cartographic Museum) in the palace; the rary, located in what used to be a chapel; and the old fortress with armoury where three conspirators were incarcerated during the njuração Mineira (Minas Gerais Conspiracy, see below) in 1791, luding the celebrated Portuguese-born poet Tomás Antônio Gon-a. Note that the armoury was built in 1765 to resemble a chapel h the aim of deceiving the enemy about the real function of the , thus reducing the chances of being bombarded.

Although the museum with its displays of Brazilian mapmaking ls isn't particularly stimulating, the tour provides insight into the eral charm of the place, its historical character and the lovely pan-mic views over the city.

In 1905 Archbishop Arcoverde, in residence at the Bishop's Palace, s appointed as the first Latin American cardinal.

The palace itself stands over the remains of a small monastery built 1669 by French Capuchin monks, who were expelled from Brazil in)1. Previously (in 1655), a hermitage built on the site in 1634 had n ceded to the Carmelite order.

In 1923, after the new official residence of the Bishops of Rio lácio São Joaquim) was constructed at Glória in 1918, the Con-ção palace, which had been standing empty, was bought by the ⁊y.

The Conjuração Mineira was an unsuccessful Brazilian separatist novement against the Portuguese colonisers that arose in 1789 n Minas Gerais. The rebellion was led by Tiradentes, who was denounced and captured in Rio on 10 May 1789 (see p. 14).

The world's largest port of entry for slaves

It is estimated that half of all the African slaves deported to the American continent arrived via Brazil, which received about four million slaves over the three centuries in which slavery was practised in the country. In the 19th century, the Valongo Wharf saw the transfer of between 500,000 and 1 million slaves, making it the largest port of entry for slaves in the world. Estimates suggest that until slavery was abolished, Rio alone received 20% of all the African slaves who reached the American continent alive. This makes the city and Valongo Wharf landmarks in what was the largest deportation in human history. The Valongo Wharf, which forms part of the historical and archaeological tour celebrating the city's African heritage, "was built for receiving and marketing slaves. After the arrival of the Portuguese court in Rio, in 1808, this trade became inconvenient as people were being sold in the street, dressed in pieces of cloth covering their crotches, people being sold like animals [...]", explains the historian of Africa, Alberto da Costa e Silva. Constructed in 1811, the wharf was closed in 1831 and altered to receive Teresa Cristina, Princess of the Two Sicilies, who later married Dom Pedro II. This is why it is also known as the Empress Wharf. The wharf was backfilled in 1911 as part of the renovation work undertaken in the city. During excavations in the port area in 2011 and 2012, remains from the African slave period were discovered. "We found an extensive material culture belonging to the ruling classes and African slaves. The area was steeped in Black culture and became known as Little Africa" (a nickname given to it by the composer and samba player, Heitor dos Prazeres), according to archaeologist Tania Andrade Lima. There are other sites in Rio that form part of the tour celebrating the city's African heritage: the Hanging Garden of Valongo, laid out at the beginning of the 20th century in order to wipe out all traces of the slave trade, located on the western side of the Conceição district on Rua do Camerino; the Largo do Depósito, present-day Praça dos Estivadores, at the entrance to Rua Barão de São Felix; the Pedra do Sal (Rock of Salt), Rua Argemiro Bulcão, at the foot of the Conceição district, a full-fledged monument to historical and religious tradition, where samba concerts are held every week; the José Bonifácio Cultural Centre, at 80 Rua Pedro Ernesto, an outreach and exploration centre for Black culture, housed in a (now completely restored) building, opened in 1876 by Dom Pedro II as the first public (state) school in Latin America; and the Pretos Novos Cemetery (Cemetery of the New Blacks), at 36 Rua Pedro Ernesto, discovered by accident in 1996, which holds the remains of Blacks from Africa who died before they could be sold.

"These are human remains!"

In 1996, Merced Guimarães, Director of the "Pretos Novos" Institute (see opposite), unearthed a genuine archaeological site buried in his house: "The house needed work. On the first day, the builder came and said that the previous owners must have had a lot of dogs, as the ground was full of bones. I took a jawbone and noticed that it did not come from a dog but was a human bone! The police then visited, along with the archaeologists, and they decided that this was the location of the Pretos Novos Cemetery."

"For the English to see..."

In 1831, the Valongo Wharf was closed following the banning of the transatlantic slave trade, under pressure from Great Britain. The regulation was arrogantly ignored, however, and became known ironically as the "Para inglês ver" law ("For the English to see"), an expression still used today to describe something that exists solely for the sake of appearances. The slave trade with Brazil was genuinely halted with the signing of the Eusébio de Queirós law in 1850, although the last known expedition dates from 1872 and slavery persisted until it was finally abolished in 1888.

Valongo Wharf was declared part of the national heritage in November 2013, when UNESCO determined that the site was part of the "Slave Route", a project inaugurated by the organisation in 2006 in order to highlight the tangible and intangible heritage of the global slave trade. In 2016, the UNESCO World Heritage Centre accepted Valongo Wharf's application to be categorised as world heritage.

DI CAVALCANTI FRESCOES ON THE NEWSROOM

Painting for the visually impaired

Centro Cultural Light – Avenida Marechal Floriano 168
(21) 2211-4515 – ccl@light.com.br
Monday to Friday, 11am–5pm
Admission free
Metro: Presidente Vargas

Rio's downtown Light Cultural Centre, four panels of a series of five y the celebrated modernist painter Di Cavalcanti, featuring the press at rk, can be 'seen' by the visually impaired. Along with Portuguese and ille captions that explain the artwork, there are bas-reliefs that let blind ple understand the design of each panel by running their hands over all marble reproductions.

The main component of *Composition Rio* – as the entire work is wn – is the reporter, represented by a man with two faces turned in osite directions, intent on turning facts and figures into news. This ality is symbolised by the Sun and the Moon, expressing the pressure ime on the journalist's day. On these panels – restored to perfect con- on – Di Cavalcanti's vibrant aesthetic sense and use of many colours ture the intense pace of the newsroom, underlining the importance of press to society. He also showcases the diversity of information and ple's reactions to it, the role of the law and the diversity of Brazilian ture.

The artist was commissioned for these panels by Samuel Wainer, nder and owner of the daily *Última hora* (At the Last Minute) based in , to celebrate the newspaper's first anniversary in 1952. They were kept he office until 1970 when Wainer, who was in financial difficulties, put m up for sale.

Four of the panels were bought by Light. Displayed in various places r the years, they are now on permanent exhibition in a special room he Light Cultural Center, opened in mid-2014. A photo of the fifth el is also shown.

---

miliano Augusto Cavalcanti de Albuquerque e Melo (1897– 976), a major modernist painter, draftsman, illustrator and cari- aturist, was the director of the Semana de Arte Moderna (Week f Modern Art) in 1922. A friend of Picasso, Matisse and Jean Cocteau, known as the "Métis painter", Di Cavalcanti said: *"I ouldn't live without Rio de Janeiro, for everything that I see as a pain- er is part of the Carioca landscape".*

Última Hora was a benchmark in Brazilian journalism through its echnical and graphic innovations. In the words of Samuel Wainer t was "a newspaper in opposition to the ruling class and in favour f a government" (that of Getúlio Vargas). Founded on 12 June 951, it was sold to the *Folha de São Paulo* in 1971 and finally topped publication in 1991.

STATUE OF SÃO DISMAS

A rare image of the penitent thief crucified with Jesus

Igreja de São Gonçalo Garcia e São Jorge
Rua da Alfândega 382
Monday to Friday 7am–4.30pm, Saturday 7.30am–11.30am,
Sunday 8am–11am
Metro: Presidente Vargas

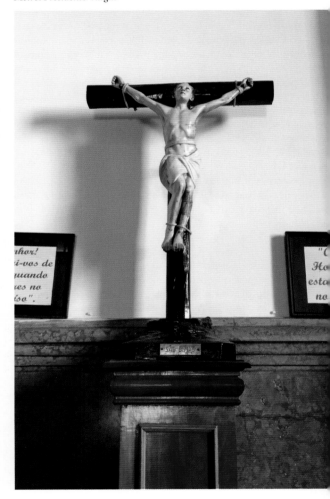

o the right of the main entrance of the church dedicated to St Gonçalo Garcia and St George, the sharp-eyed visitor will spot the statue
a crucified man. Unlikely as it seems, this doesn't represent Christ: the
ne of São Dimas (St Dismas) is given at the foot of the cross.

Although his name doesn't appear in the New Testament canon, it
es in the apocryphal Gospel of Nicodemus, the disciple who helped
eph of Arimathea with the descent from the Cross and the entomb-
nt of Christ.

Dismas, whose feast day is celebrated on 12 October in the East and
March in the West, was the first saint in the Church's history, canon-
d for having converted on the cross just before dying. While Dismas,
rist and Gesmas (the impenitent thief, whose name also appears in
: Gospel of Nicodemus) were already on the cross, Gesmas began to
nt Jesus: "Are you not the Christ? Save yourself and us."

Dismas then rebuked Gesmas: "Don't you fear God, since you are
der the same sentence? We are punished justly, for we are getting
at our deeds deserve: but this man has done nothing wrong." He
ded: "Jesus, remember me when you come into your Kingdom."
ving repented of his sins and recognised Jesus as the Saviour, Christ

d him just before he died:
ou will be with me in Par-
ise" (Luke 23:40–43).

Dismas is also tradition-
y mentioned during the
ght to Egypt as one of
o bandits who robbed the
oly Family of their money
d their donkey. Moved by
eir poverty on the road to
le, Dismas returned their
operty. The Child Jesus
anked him, promising
at he would remember
m, which he did at the
ucifixion.

LAGARTO FOUNTAIN ON RUA FREI CANECA

A forgotten lizard

Corner of Rua Frei Caneca and Rua Salvador de Sá
Metro: Praça Onze

t the point where Rua Frei Caneca crosses Rua Salvador de Sá
and skirts the hill, opposite the police station on one side and the
nbódromo on the other, it's easy to miss the lizard at the centre of a
he that was part of the region's water supply.

The water gushing from the lizard's jaws was collected in a basin,
w overgrown with plants that cover – and protect – the lizard. This
t the original bronze, but a steel copy.

At the centre of the structure, an oval panel bears a Latin phrase:
enti populu – senatus profusit aquas – anno MDCCLXXXVI ("to the
rsty people the senate gave abundant water in the year 1786"). The
graved inscription fails to mention the sculptor of the little reptile,
ich is attributed to Mestre Valentim (1745–1813).

Thanks to the lizard's capacity to regrow its tail, and because it hiber-
es, the reptile is associated with healing and resurrection, also linked
the waters of the fountain.

EARBY
useu da Polícia militar do Estado do Rio de ⑧
neiro

a Marques de Pombal 128 – (21) 2332-6668 / 2242-4059
esday to Thursday 9am–4pm (admission free)

o minutes' walk from the lizard fountain, the Military Police Muse-
, housed in a beautiful 19th-century mansion, has objects and docu-
nts relating to the history of Rio's police forces. Key exhibits include
armour collection from the 15th and 16th centuries brought over
the Portuguese crown in 1808, some antique weapons, and a room
voted to the Paraguay War complete with a stuffed dog that took part
the conflict.

FACADE OF THE FORMER LAMBERT PERFUME AND SOAP FACTORY

A stunning yet forgotten facade

Rua do Senado 244–246 – Metro: Central

orgotten in Rua do Senado, the blue and white facade at number 244–246 is one of the most charming in the city and in very good ndition. The first floor has a remarkable sculpture of a woman, holg a hammer resting on an anvil in her right hand, and in her left d a set square and compass.

Built in 1920, the building once housed the former Lambert perne and soap factory, as told by photographer and historian Luiz gênio Teixeira Leite in his extraordinary book, *O Rio que o Rio não vê* e Rio that Rio Doesn't See). In one sense, the hammer and anvil refer the former industrial activity (production of consumer goods). The are and compass, which on the face of it, symbolise the architect's rk, are also Masonic symbols.

For Freemasons, the compass symbolises the Spirit, whereas the are (symbol of Matter) indicates "righteousness in action". When th tools are linked, they express the balance between spiritual and maial forces, a necessary condition to achieve spiritual enlightenment. is enlightenment is represented in the Masonic hierarchy by the 3rd de of Master Mason, where the compass is placed on the square (as e), indicating that spirituality has *conquered* matter.

Is this the meaning of the laurel crown (symbol of victory) on the ue's head?

Similarly, the large shell carved above the woman is often, by its very m, associated with the female sexual organ. Its presence would also all the victory of the spirit over human sexual (material) instincts.

MUSEU DA POLÍCIA CIVIL WAXWORKS

Museum open despite renovations

Rua da Relação 40
museu@pcerj.rj.gov.br
Monday to Friday 10.30am–5pm

The Civil Police Museum isn't closed to the public, despite the er[...] less work being carried out in the superb main building, dati[...] from 1910. However, not all the historical collection is on display, [...] objects associated with spiritualist cults or Candomblé are in storage[...]

In addition to weapons and uniforms, the exhibits include some [...] table fake documents as well as Dr Alberto Baldissara's impressive v[...] reproductions of faces and body parts.

The idea was to preserve the traces of violent crimes as realistically [...] possible, to help the forensic teams.

IGHT ARM OF NOSSA SENHORA ⑪
OS PRAZERES' STATUE

saint persecuted by thieves

eja de Santo Antônio dos Pobres
a dos Inválidos 42 (corner of Rua do Senado)
) 2222-2586
nday to Friday 7.30am–5pm, Saturday 7.30am–12pm,
iday 7am–12pm
mission free
s: 126, 161, 201, 433, 464

he first side altar to the right as you enter the church of St Anthony
of the Poor is dedicated to Nossa Senhora dos Prazeres (Our Lady
the Pleasures).

Her statue used to stand in the oratory bearing her name at Arco
Teles, Praça XV de Novembro, in the 18th century. Around 1830 it
s moved here by a believer, Manoel Machado de Oliveira, to save it
m the alcoholics, thieves and vandals who frequented the area around
raça Quinze", as the square is generally known.

Somewhat ironically, in 2013 a thief up to his usual tricks broke the
inedglass window behind the small altar and snapped off the statue's
ht arm as he clambered into the church.

The statue was repaired but the restored arm has been left unpaint-
as a reminder of this lamentable deed, as any keen-eyed visitor will
tice. Moreover, the replacement glass is completely at odds with the
t of the window.

The original Baroque church was consecrated in 1811. In 1831, as
e church had grown too small and was in a poor state of repair, anoth-
was built in the same style.

This was restored in 1854, using slaked
ne and concrete slabs for the flooring.
ut the constant floods in the area dam-
ed the foundations and walls, which is
ny a new church – the third – was built
the same location between 1940 and
49 in a neo-Romanesque style. The
ined-glass windows depicting the life
St Anthony are installed 1.20 m above
eet level to prevent flooding.

RAISED FLOOR OF IGREJA DO SANTÍSSIMO SACRAMENTO DA ANTIGA SÉ

Short slaves in their place at Mass

Avenida Passos 50
Monday to Friday 8am–4.30pm, Sunday 8.30am–2pm
Metro: Central

ntering the church of the Holy Sacrament of the Old Cathedral, you don't immediately spot the slightly raised section (measuring er 3 or 4 m) of the 19th-century tiled flooring in the nave.

Despite what you might think, nobody's buried beneath the floor. is area was purposely raised so that the shorter slaves (those below 6 m) could stand and watch Mass being celebrated. The taller slaves d to stand at the back.

As this church was consecrated in 1859, and slavery wasn't abolished til the Lei Áurea (Golden Law) of 1888, the slaves at the time would and at the back.

Seated in front were the bourgeoisie and merchants, then on the left e *fazendeiros* (farmers) and on the right religious brotherhoods, such the Santíssimo Sacramento da Antiga Sé, founded between 1567 and 69, which built this church.

Note that the last three rows of the farmers' pews have a small but nificant detail – engraved at the entrance to each is an "X", two "Xs" three "Xs", depending on the wealth of their *fazendas*.

The brotherhoods' pews are kewise engraved with the Ro-an numerals I, II and III, sig-fying their degree of affluence.

The nobility took part in ass from the first floor, seated the lodges that can still be en on either side of the choir.

The church also boasts the dest baptismal font in Rio. own at the far right, don't iss the charming chapel of ossa Senhora da Piedade (Our dy of Piety), where the ceiling unfortunately disintegrating.

CASA FRANKLIN FACADE

A hundred-year-old peacock

Avenida Passos 36
Metro: Central

Number 36 Avenida Passos, just a few steps from the Igreja de San-
tissimo Sacramento da Antiga Sé (Church of the Holy Sacrament
the Old Cathedral), is one of the city's architectural gems. But in a
sy street with relatively narrow sidewalks it's easy to walk past this
11 building without even noticing it.

The spectacular facade features thirteen French stained-glass win-
ws that form a large peacock's tail. Each "feather" bears a letter which,
en combined, spell the name Casa Franklin. This intricate facade,
h its Art Nouveau elements, is topped by a bronze eagle holding a
np in its beak. The building, which was originally an electrical and
rdware store, can now be hired as a venue for large functions and
rties.

EARBY

Iuseu da Bíblia

a Buenos Aires 135
mday to Friday 9am–6pm

n the first floor of a religious book store, a canopy-covered space hous-
a small museum dedicated to the Bible. There are some interesting
planations about the origins of the Bible and the fact that it has been
inslated into more than 2,300 languages (the museum has a copy in
iaraní and one in Tupana Ehay, the language of an Indian tribe from
rthern Brazil). Other unusual items include a stone from Mount Si-
i, two containers of water from the Dead Sea, and especially (children
ve this) perfumes from biblical times that you can smell, like the Ma-
s famous myrrh.

DI CAVALCANTI PANELS
AT THE JOÃO CAETANO THEATRE

Brazil's first two modernist paintings

Teatro João Caetano
Praça Tiradentes
Open during performances
Metro: Carioca

he first-floor foyer of the João Caetano Theatre – originally built in 1813 and extensively renovated over the following two centuries – the hiding place of two valuable panels by Di Cavalcanti painted in on mortarboard, dating from 1929.

These paintings, entitled *Samba* and *Carnaval*, are barely known to cariocas: the foyer behind the first-floor balcony is little used, despite e posters tracing the history of the theatre and the fact that visitors ve to pass through there to find the toilets.

The paintings themselves have been restored a number of times, ost recently in 1995.

Strongly influenced by Mexican muralists José Clemente Orozco d David Alfaro Siqueiros, the panels depict mixed-race characters ncing the samba to the sound of the flute, *pandeiro* (a kind of tam-urine), tambourine, guitar and *cavaquinho* (a small guitar). These are obably Brazil's first two modernist paintings. From the 1920s, this ovement sought to go back to the Brazilian roots of music, literature d the arts in general.

This decade was a fertile period that saw the emergence of Emiliano Cavalcanti, Cândido Portinari and Tarsila (do Amaral) in the visual ts, poets Carlos Drummond de Andrade and Manuel Bandeira, and iters Jorge Amado, Graciliano Ramos and Raquel de Queiroz, as well the music of Villa-Lobos. Brazil widened its horizons and incorporat-creative aspects of other regions of the country in the Rio–São Paulo is. In this atmosphere, the manifold talents of Di Cavalcanti, thinker, lker" and artist, flourished.

Di Cavalcanti (1897–1976), who was born in Rio de Janeiro, even rote a book that reflects his personality and his love for the city: *miniscências líricas de um perfeito carioca* (Lyrical Reminiscences of Perfect Carioca). He loved the daily life of the city and sought to present the passion he felt for the rhythmic movements of samba, the lourful magic of Carnaval and the "dangerous" curves of women of ixed descent, a recurring theme in his painting.

STATUE OF JOÃO CAETANO

A shifting statue

Teatro João Caetano
Praça Tiradentes
Metro: Carioca

he statue of actor João Caetano dos Santos, opposite the João Caetano Theatre, originally stood in front of the nearby Academia Im-
rial de Belas Artes (Imperial Academy of Fine Arts). The statue was
ved in 1916, during renovation work carried out by the Banco do
asil. The actor is dressed as Oscar, Son of Ossian, one of his best-
own roles.

For more about the theatre, see next page.

Remains of the Academia Imperial de Belas Artes

Opened in 1826, the Imperial Academy of Fine Arts was considered
o be the most beautiful building in Rio. Designed by the "father" of
rchitectural teaching in Brazil, Grandjean de Montigny, it was de-
nolished in 1938. Nothing has yet been built in its place, incredible
s that may sound... Besides the João Caetano statue, the Academy's
ntrance gate was preserved and is now at the Botanical Garden (see
. 112).

he last vestige, which is more subtle, is the semicircular plaza at the
orner of Travessa das Belas Artes and Rua Imperatriz Leopoldina.
Although Montigny had wanted to build the plaza since 1836 to
rovide a better view of the Academy, especially its magnificent
ateway, it wasn't finished until 1847. Rua Imperatriz Leopoldina
as opened three years later, in 1850, the first "circular square" in
razil.

The curse of Teatro João Caetano

In 1813, the João Caetano Theatre was partly built with stones originally intended for the cathedral in Largo de São Francisco de Paula (now the Institute of Philosophy and Social Sciences, nearby). As the latter work was interrupted, the stones were reused for the theatre foundations. Some saw this as sacrilegious and the origins of the curse on the theatre, which suffered three fires in less than thirty years: in 1824, 1831 and 1839.

Demolished and rebuilt in Art Deco style in 1928 (see photo), the theatre was again completely restored in 1978 to become what it is today.

For some, the present building is an architectural carbuncle in the heart of the city and the curse that hovers over it is omnipresent – how

lse to explain the fact that after being built in four different but equally attractive styles (three classical and one Art Deco), its current confi-
guration is so unharmonious? Wouldn't the solution be to demolish
it once and for all to open up the view between Praça Tiradentes and
the Real Gabinete Real da Leitura (a library with a vast collection of
volumes by Portuguese authors)?

Rent-a-slave for an evening at the theatre...

In the colonial era, the theatre was a longstanding status symbol – it
was a good thing to be seen there with slaves to show your importance.
People who had no slaves could even hire them for the evening to give
the impression of wealth.

GOLDEN ROSE OF THE MUSEU ARQUIDIOCESANO DE ARTE SACRA

The princess's Golden Rose

Museu Arquidiocesano de Arte Sacra
Catedral Metropolitana de São Sebastião – Avenida República do Chile 245
Wednesday 9am–12pm and 1pm–4pm, Saturday and Sunday 9am–12pm
Other days, visits on reservation only, call (21) 2240-2669 / 2240-2869 /
2262-1797 (free access to cathedral 8am–5pm daily)
Metro: Carioca

The well-hidden (and seldom visited) Archdiocesan Museum of Sacred Art in the cathedral basement has a collection of over 5,000 pieces of religious art. Among them is a very special work.

At the back of the museum, on the left, curious visitors will find a Golden Rose presented by Pope Leo XIII (1810–1903) to Princess Isabel (1846–1921), daughter of Emperor Pedro II and acting regent of the Empire of Brazil. The rose, or rather bunch of roses, consists of a cm stem with 12 branches, 24 thorns, 12 buds and 124 leaves. It rests in a neoclassical silver vase.

On 29 May 1888, a few days after the princess had signed the Lei Áurea (Golden Law) of 13 May that abolished slavery (Brazil was the last independent American country to free its slaves), Leo XIII signed

the letter granting the Golden Rose. As he said to Isabel: "Do not look at the price of the object and value, but be attentive to the most sacred mystery it represents."

He also stressed that the flower symbolises the majesty of Christ, and its fragrance "remotely permeates all those who scrupulously emulate its virtues".

The Golden Rose of Princess Isabel was kept by the Brazilian imperial family and donated to the Metropolitan Cathedral to mark the centenary of the birth of the princess.

What is the Golden Rose?

The Golden Rose is a sacred ornament that usually depicts a single rose (sometimes a spray of roses) in solid gold. Every year, the pope would present one to a sovereign, a place of worship or pilgrimage, or even an entire community, as a special mark of honour. Since many of these precious objects were subsequently melted down for their gold, only a few rare examples still exist: one in the Treasury of the Basilica of St Marks in Venice, one in the Musée de Cluny in Paris, one in the Palazzo Comunale of Siena (Tuscany), two in the Treasury of the Hofburg in Vienna, one in the Treasury of the Cathedral of Benevento (southern Italy) and one in the Museum of Sacred Art in the Vatican Library. More recent popes (including John Paul II) have presented Golden Roses to Lourdes, to the Brazilian basilica of Nossa Senhora Aparecida (1967 and 2007) and to the Sanctuary of Guadalupe (Mexico). Although the first mention of such a Golden Rose was in 1049, in a papal bull issued by Pope Leo IX, the earliest mention of one being presented by a pope dates from the end of the 11th century: in 1098–1099, Urban II gave one to Count Foulques d'Anjou for preaching the First Crusade. As the message that always accompanies it makes clear, the Golden Rose is a secular honour with spiritual significance. Just as the rose is considered the most beautiful and highly perfumed of all flowers, its presentation as a gift expresses the pontiff's wish that the heart and spirit of the recipient will be bathed in an equally divine fragrance.

The slab of concrete from Galeão runway that Pope John Paul II kissed

There are two other eye-catching pieces in the museum collection. When John Paul II came to Rio for the first time, he kissed the ground as usual on alighting at Galeão International Airport on 1 July 1980. This piece of the runway is now in the museum. In a showcase near this exhibit is the "Pope's ring". When the pope went through the *favela* of Vidigal during the same papal visit, he took the gold ring off his finger and donated it to the community. Since 1982, it has been part of the museum collection. The Archdiocese has had a silver replica made, which was displayed in the chapel of São Francisco de Assis (St Francis of Assisi), built by Vidigal residents as a joint project for the pope's visit. The replica ring was stolen years later and a new one made.

AZULEJOS AT THE CLUBE DOS DEMOCRÁTICOS

Three delightful and little-known panels

Rua do Riachuelo 93 – Metro: Cinelândia

he upper facade of the Democrats Club headquarters – built in 1930 by Sebastião Oliveira, and one of the major Carnaval schools the early decades of the 20th century – features three delightful and le-known *azulejo* panels.

Themes include Pierrot and Columbine and two chorus girls talking Charlie Chaplin. The design is attributed to cartoonist Trinas Fox.

In the lobby, pretty female figures in polychrome stucco relief show cers clad in brief costumes, highlighting the carnival theme.

The front entrance, with its geometric lines and refined aesthetics, o demonstrates the marriage between carnival caricatures and the camlined architecture typical of a modern metropolis.

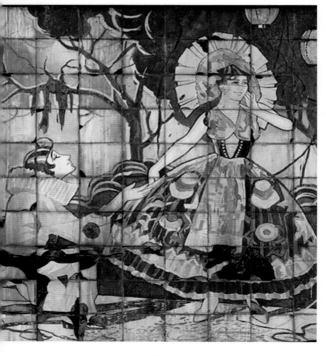

ESCOLA DE MÚSICA CONCERT HALL

One of the city's finest interiors

Rua do Passeio 98
musica.ufrj.br
Occasionally open to the public, free concerts
Metro: Cinelândia

Although the Rio Music School building (next to the Automobile Club) is well known to Cariocas, few have crossed its threshold. Which is a pity, because its lovely facade leads to one of the city's finest interiors, with a delightfully old-fashioned atmosphere.

To see inside, take a look at the programme of free concerts regularly held there.

One of the monumental staircases will take you first of all to the charming foyer facing the entrance to the concert hall. This room is worth a visit: its terrace has a delightful and unusual view of downtown Rio. The main attraction, however, is the group of four beautiful frescoes on the theme of music, executed in 1922 by Brazilian artist and designer Antônio Parreiras. The Art Nouveau style of "*Osiris – Inventor of the Flute*" and "*Seven Notes*" is particularly successful.

The concert hall itself, inspired by the Salle Gaveau (former headquarters of the famous piano makers in Paris), is one of the largest in the country and known for its excellent acoustics.

With the proclamation of the Republic in 1889, the former conservatory, dating from 1848, became a national music institute. The first director was composer Leopoldo Miguez (1850–1902), who gave his name to the concert hall.

On his appointment, he travelled to Europe to visit various conservatories and observe different teaching methods. The institute moved in 1913 and the present building dates from 1922.

INVERNO STATUE
IN THE PASSEIO PÚBLICO

A statue disappears then reappears, sanctified

Entrance via Rua do Passeio, between Lapa and Cinelândia
Open daily
Free
Metro: Cinelândia

The *Inverno* (Winter) statue in the Passeio Público, originally veiled in 1861 along with three other works (together represent the four seasons), disappeared for a good part of the 20th century.

The statue was eventually found in 2000 in the gardens of the Cen Cultural Municipal Laurinda Santos Lobo, Santa Tereza, and repla in the public park the same year. It's said that when the statue of "saint" was removed from the cultural centre, local devotees made curious request that she should remain there as they now worship Nossa Senhora de Ferro (Our Iron Lady), as they called her.

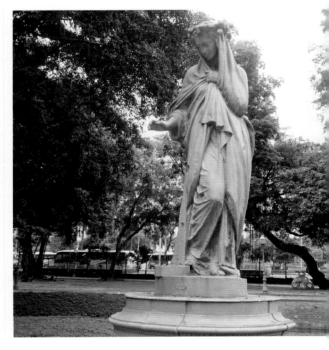

A foul smell that led to the park being renovated

The Passeio Público, the public park built in the 18th century in the style of a French formal garden by Mestre Valentim da Fonseca e Silva (1745–1813), underwent a major renovation after the embarrassing experience of Prince Maximilian of Austria in January 1860. Strolling along the terrace, with its pavilions offering magnificent views over Guanabara Bay, he couldn't stand the overpowering stench and held his nose with a handkerchief. So Dom Pedro II decided to renovate the park and French botanist and landscaper Auguste Glaziou (1833–1906) – called the "landscaper of the empire" for his many projects in Rio – was commissioned for the job. With Glaziou, the gardens reverted to the English style. He cut down a number of trees and replanted other large species that are still there today, and installed the four seasons statues, cast at Val d'Osne in France.

Seaview

The Passeio Público was built on land reclaimed from the lagoon of Boqueirão da Ajuda, considered a "pestilential swamp". Lying beside Guanabara Bay, its banks were very busy. With the opening of Avenida Beira-Mar in 1906, however, the site was further from the shore, and even further away after Aterro do Flamengo was reclaimed from the sea in 1965.

Remains of a fountain recalling the viceroy's forbidden love

At the far end of the park is all that remains of the Fonte dos Amores (Love Fountain). This fountain, designed by Mestre Valentim, was thought to have been inspired by the passion of Viceroy Luís de Vasconcelos (1742–1809) for Suzana, a poor girl who lived in a shack at the edge of the lagoon. Elements of the fountain, also known as Fonte dos Jacarés (Crocodile Fountain), symbolise the characters in his romance. Two centuries later, it was the inspiration for the Portela samba school, who sang about the "Carioca Legend: Dreams of the Viceroy" at the 1988 Carnaval. The Crocodile Fountain, the two granite pyramids facing it and the entrance gate are the criteria under which the Passeio Público is classified as national heritage.

Inaugurated in 1783, almost a hundred years before New York's Central Park, the Passeio Público was the first public park in the Americas.

SECRETS OF
THE INSTITUTO HISTÓRICO
E GEOGRÁFICO BRASILEIRO

The oldest waymarker in Brazil, a foundlings' whee
and a spectacular view...

Avenida Augusto Severo 8
ihgb.org.br – (21) 2252-4430 / 2509-5107
Monday to Friday 1pm–5pm (reservations by phone)
Admission free
Metro: Cinelândia

Book a visit to the Brazilian Historical and Geographical Instit
(IHGB), housed in a central building in the Glória neighbourho
to appreciate some of its interesting and little-known aspects.

The *salão nobre* (great hall) holds a historical treasure: the Marco
Cananéia – the oldest waymarker in Brazil. This type of stone mar
carved with a flared cross (cross pattée, like that of the Knights Temp
and the shield of Portugal, was used to designate regions where Jesuits
settled. The stones were originally used as ballast by the caravels that sai
from Portugal to Brazil laden with precious timber. This one is though
have been set up on Ilha do Cardoso (near Cananéia and the other isla
of a small archipelago on the south coast of São Paulo) by the expedit
commanded by Gaspar de Lemos that landed there on 24 January 15
The navigator and cartographer was the Italian Amerigo Vespucci, w
was honoured by having the newly discovered continent named after h
The stone was found at Ponta do Itacuruçá and transported to the IH
in the mid 19th-century. A replica is kept on Cardoso.

On the 12th floor of the museum is a foundlings' wheel that was ginally installed at Rua Evaristo da Veiga, next to the military police racks. Any children abandoned there were handed over to the San- Casa da Misericórdia in Rua Santa Luzia (for more on foundlings' eels see p. 155).

Finally, the terrace on the 13th floor offers a spectacular view of the ectic architecture of the city centre.

Cananéia is considered to be the oldest settlement in Brazil. Marataiama (its original name) was founded by Portuguese explorer and colonial administrator Martim Afonso de Souza in 1531. As there is no documentary evidence to prove this, some claim that the country's first city was São Vicente, whose archives confirm that it was founded on 22 January 1532, also by Afonso de Souza.

Unfinished painting of Pedro II's coronation

The great hall also features a very special painting. On the back vall hangs an unfinished canvas entitled Coroação de Pedro II Coronation of Pedro II) by Manuel de Araújo Porto Alegre (1806– 879). He began the painting just after the coronation in July 1841, ut as the government failed to confirm that it would buy the work, e never finished it. Curiously enough, the following year, Pedro II lecorated the French painter François-René Moreaux (1807–1860) o reward him for his painting also depicting the coronation (now lisplayed in the Museu Imperial de Petrópolis). The unfinished anvas was stored in the cellar of the Escola Nacional de Belas Artes National School of Fine Arts, now National Museum of Fine Arts) or almost a century before coming to the IHGB.

otafogo – Flamengo – Laranjeiras – Catete – Gloria – Sta Teresa

1. BAS-RELIEF STATUE OF SÃO SEBASTIÃO — 118
2. GETÚLIO VARGAS MEMORIAL — 120
3. MEMORIAL COMMEMORATING THE OPENING OF THE PORTS IN 1808 — 122
4. VILLINO SILVEIRA DOORWAY — 124
5. MONUMENT TO THE CARIOCA RIVER — 126
6. GRUTA DE LOURDES, IGREJA DA SANTISSIMA TRINDADE — 130
7. MORRO DA VIÚVA — 132
8. CASA MARAJOARA — 136
9. STAINED-GLASS WINDOWS AT FLUMINENSE FOOTBALL CLUB — 138
10. PALÁCIO GUANABARA — 140
11. GRAVEYARD OF THE "LITTLE ANGELS" — 142
12. TOMB OF THE MARQUIS OF PARANÁ — 144
13. STAINED-GLASS WINDOW COMMEMORATING THE NAVY DEAD — 146
14. PROJETO MORRINHO — 148
15. SOCIEDADE BUDISTA DO BRASIL — 150
16. FORMER VATICAN EMBASSY IN RIO — 151
17. RUSSIAN ORTHODOX CHURCH OF ST ZINAIDA — 152
18. THE REMAINS OF THE SANTA TERESA CABLE CAR — 153
19. FOUNDLINGS' WHEELS, CARMELITE CONVENTO DE SANTA TERESA — 154
20. ACADEMIA BRASILEIRA DE LITERATURA DE CORDEL — 156

BAS-RELIEF STATUE
OF SÃO SEBASTIÃO

The miraculous appearance of St Sebastian

Praça Luís de Camões (also known as Largo do Russel)
Metro: Glória

Although Cariocas are well aware of the statue of São Sebastião (St Sebastian) in Largo do Russel, few realise its significance.

It was here, in July 1566, that the Portuguese soldiers led by Estácio Sá claimed that St Sebastian had appeared. Thanks to this divine ervention, the Portuguese defeated the French at the famous battle s Canoas" (of the canoes).

The following year, on 20 January (the saint's feast day), victory at e battle of Uruçu-mirim (near where Morro da Glória church now nds) consolidated the Portuguese presence and resulted in the expul- n of the French from the island colony known as France Antarctique. tácio de Sá was seriously wounded by an arrow, just like St Sebastian, tron of the city, and died a month later from his injuries.

The battle of the canoes and belief in the intervention of St Sebastian immortalised on the base of the statue, a bas-relief depicting a battle ne, with the title "Apparition of St Sebastian at the Battle against the noes". Just below is an inscription that translates as: "Just to be called y of St Sebastian is to be favoured by the Lord and by the merits of e Glorious Martyr."

The 7 m statue by sculptor Dante Crossi was erected in 1965, in mmemoration of the fourth centenary of the founding of the city.

The representation of the saint hanging from a tree trunk, wounded three arrows, is inspired by a statue of St Sebastian brought to Rio de eiro in the 16th century.

Portuguese sailors were the first to discover anabara Bay on 1 January 1502. Believing e entrance to the bay to be the mouth of a er, they named it Rio de Janeiro.

It was only in March 1565 that the city was nded, upon the arrival of Estácio de Sá to ack the French. It was given the name "São bastião do Rio de Janeiro" in homage to the en king of Portugal, Dom Sebastião.

© Eugenio Hansen

At the time that the city was founded, Glória hill sometimes resem- bled an island as there were so many sources of water in the region. Just opposite was a beach, later named Praia do Russel (before it was built over), as well as a swamp (which became Largo da Glória after landfill) and the Catete river, now also in a culvert (see p. 128).

GETÚLIO VARGAS MEMORIAL

A poignant but little-known site

Praça Luís de Camões (also known as Largo do Russel)
Tuesday to Sunday 10am–5pm
Admission free
Metro: Glória

Despite the high profile of the bust of Getúlio Vargas, 2.5 m hi and installed on a base of 3 m on Largo do Russel, it's strange th his memorial is so little known by Cariocas – perhaps because it star in a basement that can't be seen from the street and is only accessi down a discreet flight of steps. In a large quiet space, with soft ligh ing, the memorial has a permanent exhibition of photographs, texts Portuguese and English), videos and objects relating to the life of t former president and some aspects of the history of Brazil and Rio Janeiro.

During his forty-five years of public life, Getúlio Vargas lived nearly three decades in the city that was then the country's capital. Af the 1930 revolution, of which he was the main leader, Vargas was he of the interim government, President of the Republic elected by the N tional Congress, dictator and finally President of the Republic elect by the people.

The exhibition is divided into eight sections. Apart from showing
political and social context and the actions of the government of the
, they highlight Cariocas' relationship with the head of state and the
pact of government policy on the city. You can, for example, see lit-
-known photographs of urban reform undertaken during the Estado
vo (1937–1945, the period of the Vargas dictatorship); snapshots of
construction of Avenida Presidente Vargas, for which 525 buildings
4 churches were demolished; the opening of Avenida Brasil; the
nstruction of Santos Dumont Airport; and the urbanisation of Espla-
da do Castelo, where the Ministries of Finance, Labour, Education
Health (see p. 49) were built.

The final sections of the exhibition are devoted to the intense politi-
and military pressure that led Vargas to commit suicide with a bullet
ough the heart on 24 August 1954, at the nearby Catete Palace (153
a do Catete). The photos on display at the memorial as the last tribute
he president, in particular one of the crowd accompanying the funeral
cession to Santos Dumont airport, are impressive and moving.

The memorial monument stands 17.5 m high – no higher than the
reetops so as not to obstruct the neighbouring buildings' view of
he sea.

MEMORIAL COMMEMORATING THE OPENING OF THE PORTS IN 1808

The other vestige commemorating the opening of the ports in 1808

Avenida Beira Mar
Metro: Gloria

Although the centenary of the opening of the ports to friendly tions (see opposite) was celebrated with great pomp with a Natio Exposition at Urca (see p. 188), it was also commemorated in 1908 rig here beside the former Hotel Glória by two flights of ornamental steps balustrade and two statues.

The statues, by French sculptor Eugène Bénet, were inspired by the of Place de la Concorde in Paris. They represent trade (a seated wom holding a caduceus, the symbol of commerce, on the Flamengo side) a navigation (a seated woman holding an anchor in her left hand, on Largo do Russel side). At the foot of each statue, facing Rua do Russ an inscription is engraved in the stone: 28 January 1808 – opening the ports.

The date 1908 (in Roman numerals: MCMVIII) can be seen at foot of each statue, facing Avenida Beira Mar, with a small plaque expla ing the historical context.

Opening of the ports in 1808

In 1806, Napoleon had Portugal against the wall. The Portuguese prince regent (the future King João VI) was summoned to join the blockade against Great Britain, otherwise the French would invade his country. The Portuguese sovereign was faced with a dilemma: the alliance with France and joining the blockade would mean Portugal breaking with Great Britain, the end of trade with its colonies and the loss of his empire, which he could not resign himself to. This is what revived the long-standing project to transfer the Portuguese court to Brazil, proposed in 1803 by his adviser Dom Rodrigo de Sousa Coutinho.

October 1807: precipitating events, Napoleon ordered the immediate invasion of Portugal. On 18 October, General Junot crossed the French–Spanish border at the head of an army of 25,000 men on their way to Portugal. The advance went less smoothly than expected.

On 29 November, at the last moment, a Portuguese fleet of sixteen ships containing 15,000 people (the royal family, courtesans, aristocrats, the bourgeoisie, civil servants, senior officials and a considerable number of Portuguese officers) left Portugal for Brazil. The prince regent and his entourage took with them the crown art collections, the state archives, the royal treasury, and even the silverware from churches and the Royal Library. At 9am the next day, Junot arrived in the deserted Portuguese capital with his 25,000 men. The flight of the King of Portugal was facilitated by the British, on one condition: he was to decree the opening of Brazilian ports to trade as soon as possible. Until then, Brazil had only been allowed to trade with Portugal, which had a monopoly of trade with the colony (colonial pact): incredible as it may seem today, nothing could be bought or sold in Brazil without physically passing through Portugal.

On 28 January 1808, four days after his arrival in Salvador on his way to Rio, João VI signed the decree authorising the opening of the ports. This allowed goods to be traded directly with Brazil, bypassing Portugal, which was in Napoleon's hands. Although João VI obviously had no choice, the major beneficiaries of this agreement were the British, who negotiated particularly favourable customs tariffs.

At the time, the ocean reached the foot of the steps and Avenida Beira Mar, which was opened in 1906. Not until 1922, when Morro do Castelo was levelled (see p. 59), were the beaches of Santa Luzia (Castelo), Ajuda (Cinelândia), Glória, Russel and Boqueirão (opposite the Passeio Público, see p. 112) as far as Calabouço (near the National Historical Museum) built over. For more on the amount of land reclaimed by the city of Rio, see p. 56.

VILLINO SILVEIRA DOORWAY

Golden serpents doorway

Rua do Russel 734
Metro: Glória

Villino Silveira (1915), designed by the Italian architect Anto
Virzi, is one of the city's most unusual houses. It was intended
be the residence of the Elixir de Nogueira manufacturer and Cario
entrepreneur, Gervásio Renault da Silveira.

This large villa, wedged between two other buildings and quite u
like its surroundings, is perhaps Rio's best example of Art Nouve.
It features a wrought-iron gate with a cleverly executed design by t
Italian manufacturer Pagani. The handles are gilded serpents ami
profusion of rays blending sinuous and angular shapes. The hinges
the top corners, often unnoticed, are covered by what appears to b
prehistoric bird's beak in miniature.

The house, which was listed as a historic monument in 1970, w
acquired in the 1990s by the nearby Hotel Glória and converted in
a café, now closed.

"If he'd done the same in Italy, he'd have been an internationally renowned architect"

Virzi's architecture, like that of Antoni Gaudí, is unpredictable: from asymmetrical columns to fine stucco details, and window guardrails delicately worked in steel.

Arriving in Rio in 1910, Virzi was a professor at the National School of Fine Arts and designed properties for the most extravagant Carioca bourgeoisie. "If he'd done the same in Italy, he'd have been an internationally renowned architect," according to architect Alberto Taveira at the National Institute for Cultural Heritage. Unfortunately, few of his achievements survive today. Apart from this house, there are only four of his buildings in the city: Casa Villino Silveira (see opposite), the amazing Casa Villiot at Copacabana (see p. 163), Nossa Senhora de Lourdes basilica at Vila Isabel, and a warehouse at Catumbi.

The architect's other spectacular buildings have been demolished, including the Elixir de Nogueira plant (62 Rua da Glória) in 1970 and the Smith de Vasconcelos villa (680 Avenida Atlântica) in 1964.

The "miraculous" Elixir de Nogueira, the recipe for which includes walnuts, parsley, jacaranda and guaiac, dates from a time when it was believed that many diseases were caused by impurities in the blood. The elixir was advertised as a "great blood purifier".

Product labels were artistically designed and generally bore an image of its inventor, pharmacist João da Silva Silveira from Pelotas.

MONUMENT TO THE CARIOCA RIVER

Tribute to the unseen river

Praça José de Alencar
Metro: Flamengo or Largo do Machado

The first thing you'll notice on reaching Praça José de Alencar is the monument to the Brazilian novelist who gave his name to the plaza – it has stood there since 1897. To his left, with your back to the Parque do Flamengo, you'll also see a strange lamp, with a curved post attached to a concrete base. On the ground are three metallic circles of different sizes. Inside are concentric circles with two circular openings at the centre that look like spectacles, dotted with small lozenges.

If the first thing this brings to mind is upmarket manhole covers, the circles on the ground are actually the remains of little fountains (no longer working), a reminder to Cariocas that the Carioca river (see p 128–129) is flowing under their feet towards its mouth at Praia do Flamengo. This project by architect Mario Jorge Jauregui is a tribute to the forgotten river that has played such an important role in the city's history.

The redevelopment of the plaza, which saw the installation of lighting and the circles on the ground, dates from 1990 and was part of the various Rio Cidade urban planning schemes in many of the city's neighbourhoods. The controversial inclined poles at Ipanema are a well-known example from this time.

Lack of maintenance, and in some cases vandalism, have undermined the original aims, as in the case of the fountains in Praça José de Alencar.

The statue of José de Alencar, the work of Mexican sculptor Rodolfo Bernardelli (1852–1931), a naturalised Brazilian, was unveiled in 1897. On its base are carved bas-relief scenes from four of the writer's great novels: *Iracema*, *O Guarani*, *O Gaúcho* and *O Sertanejo*. Nationalism, which highlights a typically Brazilian way of feeling and thinking, is a prominent feature of his work. José de Alencar (1829–1877) was also a journalist, lawyer and politician.

Former course of the Carioca river

The source of the Carioca is in the Serra da Carioca, Tijuca forest. The river flows below Cosme Velho, Laranjeiras and Flamengo streets before it reaches the bay. Except at its source and mouth, the river can only be seen from the beautiful although poorly maintained Largo do Boticário, the small courtyard near Corcovado tram station in Cosme Velho. Its course was blocked off in the early 20th century. At one time, the Carioca divided into two at what is now Praça José Alencar (see opposite), where there was a lake. This is where the Salema bridge stood, the city's first, built by Governor António Salema between 1574 and 1577. From there, some of the water flowed towards the mouth of the river, as far as Praia do Flamengo, and the rest was diverted to the left. The branch of the river leading to Flamengo beach has survived, although it flows underground. The water is so polluted that it is treated at a plant in Flamengo park before it reaches the beach. The other branch of the river, known as the Catete, runs through a culvert under what is now Rua do Catete. It skirts the Morro da Glória to reach the sea at the former Russel beach – now built over to form a plaza with a statue of São Sebastião (St Sebastian, see p. 118) and the Memorial Municipal Getúlio Vargas (see p. 120).

Origin of the word carioca

Although there is no consensus about the origin of the word carioca, it is probably of Tupi Indian origin and refers to a stone house built in the early 16th century at Flamengo, near the mouth of the river. The Indians called it *akari oca*, i.e. the house of *acari*, which is the name of a litte fish who lives in the stone, because it was the first time the Tupi saw men live in permanent homes. The other explanation is that acari also means "catfish", the nickname given to the Portuguese because of their armour. *Akari oca* evolved into *carioca*, which became the name of the river and, over time, the word used for those born in the city.

Aqueduct, spring, fountain, plaza, street: the importance to Rio of the Carioca

The Carioca river was so important (it was used as a source of drinking water for centuries) that the name was bestowed on the places and buildings directly connected with it. The source was known as the Serra da Carioca.

The Aqueduto da Carioca (Carioca Aqueduct, generally known as the Arcos da Lapa or Lapa Arches) carried the waters of the river, diverted to Santo Antônio *morro* from Santa Teresa, to reach what later became the Chafariz da Carioca (Carioca Fountain), in Campo da Santo Antônio – the current Largo da Carioca, which is connected to Praça Tiradentes by Rua da Carioca.

The marble fountain, which has sixteen bronze spouts, was the country's first public fountain. Inaugurated in 1723 (the same year as the aqueduct), it was demolished in 1820.

The waters of the Carioca were so popular that they inspired the phrase "This is as good as Carioca water". For obvious reasons, this saying is now obsolete...

© Daneil Fuchs

GRUTA DE LOURDES, IGREJA DA SANTISSIMA TRINDADE

A reproduction of the grotto of Our Lady of Lourdes

Rua Senador Vergueiro 141
(21) 2553-3114
sstrindade.rj@gmail.com – sstrindade.com
Monday to Friday 7am–12pm and 2pm–6pm; Sunday 7.30am–12pm and 4pm–8pm

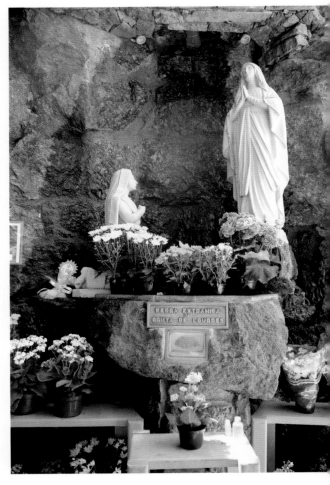

ariocas often forget about the Church of the Holy Trinity at
Flamengo, yet it has two unusual features: a lovely Art Deco fa-
le designed by French architect Henri Sajous, who worked in Brazil
ween 1930 and 1959; and, less conspicuous, a reproduction of the
ous grotto of Our Lady of Lourdes (in France), in the courtyard
ind the church.

The grotto was the brainchild of Father Aleixo Chauvin, who arrived
Rio in 1937 with a stone from Massabielle at Lourdes, where the Vir-
Mary had appeared eighteen times to Bernadette Soubirous. Father
auvin was hoping to build a replica of the famous grotto in Brazil.
nded by a Brazilian family living in France, the Rio grotto opened in
y 1939, before the present church was built. Construction began in
40 following the arrival in Rio of the Augustinians of the Assumption
1935, following the invitation of Cardinal Sebastião Leme, and was
npleted in 1945.

The congregation of Catholic brothers, also known as Assumption-
, was founded in Nimes by Father Emmanuel d'Alzon in 1845. The
le of Life adopted by the congregation draws its inspiration from that
St Augustine of Hippo. The brothers were especially devoted to the
sumption of the Virgin Mary, which explains her role in the pilgrim-
to Lourdes on 15 August (Feast of the Assumption).

As part of their mission, the Assumptionists have established replicas
the Lourdes grotto throughout the world – apart from Rio, they are
nd in Tokyo, Montreal, New York, Dublin and Milan (see *Secret
yo*, *Secret Montreal*, *Secret New York*, *Secret Dublin* and *Secret Milan*
this series of guides).

Each motif on the church's 21 stained-glass windows corresponds
o one of the 137 windows of Chartres Cathedral in France.

MORRO DA VIÚVA

One of the city's great secrets

Access by Travessa Acaraí
Metro: Botafogo

ompletely surrounded by tall buildings, Morro da Viúva (literally "Hill of the Widow") is totally hidden from the surrounding
eets. Many Cariocas don't even know it exists.

And yet, while some blocks have built-in access to the hill itself (with
orts and other facilities for the happy few living in the surrounding
ildings), there is an official secret way for the public to get onto the
orro: at the end of Avenida Oswaldo Cruz, on the Botafogo side, the
d-end street called Travessa Acaraí leads to a small door that you just
sh to open.

Don't hesitate: a Rio police chief lives at the corner and the place is
nsidered to be very safe.

The idea of accessing one of the city's truly hidden corners is espe-
lly exciting for people who are not afraid of urban exploration and
oy climbing the 195 steps that lead to the ruins of a former reservoir.

Built by Antônio Gabrielli in 1891 to supply drinking water to the
tafogo, Praia Vermelha and Leme districts, the reservoir was closed in
70 and partially listed in 1998.

Now abandoned, it's part of an area where six families leading very
gal lives will usually be happy to help you discover places with a view

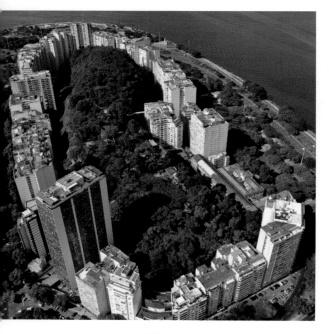

through the trees to Botafogo beach, Pedra da Gávea and Corcovado on one side, and Sugarloaf Mountain on the other.

Where does the name Morro da Viúva come from?

Morro da Viúva (Hill of the Widow) was so named in 1753, when it became the property of Dona Joaquina Figueiredo Pereira Barros on the death of her husband Joaquim José Gomes de Barros. The hill was previously named Morro do Léry, or Morro do Leryfe, after the French Protestant missionary Jean de Léry, who came to Brazil with the Huguenots under Villegaignon in the 16th century and lived in a stone house nearby.

Avenida Rui Barbosa, which skirts the *morro* on the shore side, was built in 1922.

Before the reservoir was there, fortifications had been built on this site in 1863 at a time when tensions between Brazil and Britain were high (the "Christie question", from the name of the British ambassador at the time, William Dougal Christie). The strategic and military importance of the place was soon questioned, however, and the fort was little used.

CASA MARAJOARA

The most important example of Brazilian nativist Art Deco

Rua Paissandu 319
Private residence
Metro: Flamengo

Casa Marajoara (Marajoara House) at 319 Rua Paissandu is most important example of the nativist trend in Brazilian Art D co architecture, with its direct references to indigenous influences everyday life that are still felt today.

The architectural mass of the house, a project of Gilson Gladsto Navarro dating from 1937, suggests the influence of Californian bu

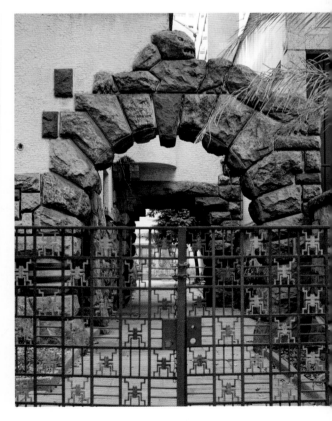

lows and North American "pueblo" architecture, but has indisputable
ces of Brazilian indigenous themes. Its nativism goes so far as to take
the name of the street (see opposite).

The cladding, which is almost entirely of polished ashlar, demon-
ates the extent to which Carioca climatic variations have been tak-
into account. In summer, a cool internal temperature is guaranteed
anks to the thick stone covering the facade. During the mild tropi-
winters, the same stone cladding provides residents with a sense of
ll-being.

There are numerous references to Amazonian talismans (see p. 175):
all the gates and iron railings, as on the interior windows, a discreet
gshaped *muiraquitã* (ancient amulet)
pears as a kind of leitmotiv. At the en-
nce, a stylised stone dragon, equally
creet, protects the place from evil.

The interior decoration of this private
idence is unique in the nativist histo-
of Brazilian Art Deco: wood panelling
sucupira (Brazilian chestnut) wood,
th motifs from Marajoara art ; ham-
ered-metal lamp fixtures that repeat
same patterns; sliding doors on which
-size portraits of Indians are etched on
glass...

Another two long-gone houses were inspired by indigenous peoples.
The first was the house in Avenida Portugal, Urca, which belonged to
Ernesto Simões Filho, Minister of Education under Getúlio Vargas.
The second was the house designed by Edgard Pinheiro Vianna on
Avenida Atlântica, known as the "house of stone". Both were demo-
lished in the late 1980s.

Rua Paissandu began at the palace where Princess Isabel and her husband, the Count of Eu (Gaston d'Orléans), lived in the 19th century.
It continued as far as Praia do Flamengo, with imperial palm trees
bordering the entire route.

The name "Paysandú" comes from a Uruguayan city that was the
scene of the historic episode known as the "taking of Paysandú" (2
January 1865) in the Paraguayan War. It involved Brazilian troops
and squadrons under General Mena Barreto (who has a street named
after him near Rua Paissandu) and Admiral Tamandaré.

STAINED-GLASS WINDOWS
AT FLUMINENSE FOOTBALL CLUB

Hidden beauty of an aristocratic club

Rua Álvaro Chaves 41
(21) 3179-7400 – fluminense.com.br
Tuesday to Friday 9am–5pm, Saturday 9am–3pm, Sunday and public holiday
9am–1pm
R$20 for non-members, R$15 for metropolitan area residents
Metro: Flamengo

members of the Fluminense Club are familiar with the beauty of their surroundings, few others know that anyone can visit this very exclusive club.

The neoclassical club building, next to Guanabara Palace (see p. 140), is the work of architect Hipólito Pujol and was opened on November 1920.

Its main salon has three beautiful stained-glass windows inspired by ancient Greece and the Roman Empire. Near the ceiling, the salon is decorated with stencils, delicate details with an intricate finish, which for years had been painted over. They were rediscovered during renovation work carried out between 2011 and 2014 and redone by hand, one by one. Also found during the restoration, beneath the ceiling paintwork, were canvases by the Timóteo da Costa brothers, who worked on the decoration of Copacabana Palace Hotel.

To the right of the club entrance, on the road leading to the tennis courts, don't miss a charming bas-relief of a tennis player in 1920s/30s style.

The ball from the first match in the Brazilian team selection

The club's trophy room (also open to the public) has an interactive exhibition showing important moments in the history of soccer in Brazil and the Fluminense Stadium, which opened in 1919 with a match between Brazil and Chile. It is on this ground that the first match in the Brazilian team selection was played on 21 July 1914 (before the opening of the stadium). The ball from the match, which was attended by 5,000 spectators, is part of the collection. The Brazilian amateurs then played against a professional team, Exeter City, from England. To everyone's surprise, Brazil won 2–0.

In 1984, the Rolling Stones recorded two video clips at the club – *Lucky in Love* and *Just Another Night*. For the first, the main salon was transformed into a casino, and for the second into a bar where you can spot an extra wearing the club's tricolour jersey. The band attended the final of the Carioca championship between Flamengo and Fluminense (Fluminense won 1–0).

PALÁCIO GUANABARA

From Empire to Republic in two hours

Rua Pinheiro Machado
(21) 2334-3774 / 2334-3216 / 2334-3215
Free guided tours on Saturdays
Reservations at visitaguiada.casacivil.rj.gov.br/VisitaGuiada
Metro: Flamengo

Many Cariocas, let alone tourists, don't know that it's possible to v Guanabara Palace, the state governor's office since 1960, when t capital was transferred to Brasília.

This neoclassical edifice – built in 1853 by Portuguese trader J Machado Coelho as a private home – was acquired by the imperial g ernment in 1865 for Princess Isabel, who had just married the Fren prince Gaston, Count of Eu. On the proclamation of the Republic 1889, the palace passed into the hands of the Union: its ownership is s disputed between the descendants of the princess and the Brazilian stat

The building has undergone several renovations over the years. T most recent, in 2011, revealed two beautiful examples of flooring fr different eras. The first, on the ground floor, where the *senzala* (roo reserved for slaves) would have been in Isabel's day, is made from stone

© Vitorhugobr

e *pé de moleque* style (see below). The well-preserved surface is covered ith glass so that visitors can appreciate the original work. The other, at e entrance to the ground floor and repeated in the veranda on the first oor, is a mosaic of ceramic tiles. These works probably date from the eat renovation of 1908, when the towers and facades were built, adding the palace's eclectic air.

The canvas hanging in the main salon, *Morte de Estácio de Sá* by Bra-ian painter and designer Antônio Parreiras, depicts some of the city unders: Estácio de Sá, Araribóia, Salvador de Sá and the Jesuit priests sé de Anchieta and Manuel da Nóbrega. In the governor's office is a desk at belonged to President Getúlio Vargas and a painting by Brazilian tist Aurélio de Figueiredo, *Abdicação de D. Pedro I*, in which the seated ild is the future Emperor Pedro II.

Behind the palace, the lovely landscaped garden, designed by French ndscaper Paul Villon, stretches almost to the forest of Corcovado.

Since Princess Isabel lived there the palace has been put to several dif-ent uses – barracks, to host illustrious guests, and the official residence the President of the Republic between 1911 and 1949, when it became e seat of the federal legislature.

Pé de moleque is a technique for laying stone flooring dating from the colonial period. One hypothesis for the origin of this name is that the work was done by young people (*moleques*), who set the stones with their feet (*pe*). Others think it's because the floor resembles an almond dessert of the same name.

In the gardens to the left of the palace is the chapel of Santa Terez-inha, built in 1946 at the request of Carmela Dutra, known as Dona Santinha, wife of President Eurico Gaspar Dutra. The altar, which is smaller than usual, was designed to allow Dona Santinha to see it from the window of her room in the palace.

In the 19th century, the main access to the palace was by Rua Pais-sandu, which was why it was planted with dozens of imperial palm trees. It's said that Princess Isabel liked to go from the palace to Flamengo beach, walking in the shade of the palms.

GRAVEYARD
OF THE "LITTLE ANGELS"

One of the most secluded and moving places in the city

Cemitério São João Batista
Rua General Polidoro / Rua Real Grandeza
Daily 9am–5pm
Metro: Botafogo

he *anjinhos* (little angels) section of St John the Baptist cemetery is one of the most secluded, mysterious, strange and moving places the entire city.

Take the main avenue after going through the main gateway on Rua neral Polidoro. About halfway to the cemetery chapel (unfortunately sed) facing you, a path heads left towards the small bare hill in the rth-east corner of the cemetery grounds, along Rua Álvaro Ramos.

At the foot of the hill, a flight of stone steps leads upwards, leaving hind the gentle murmur of the few visitors to the cemetery. The at-osphere changes very quickly: within seconds, you'll find yourself in a ested wilderness where the regular steps give way to an uneven stone :h through the undergrowth.

A few steps further and the mood changes again, ancient structures erging here and there from the tropical vegetation in an atmosphere niniscent of Colombia's "Lost City". After a few rather unsettling mo-nts, you round the final bend at the top of the hill and are faced with impressive array of white crosses stuck in the ground. Overcome by s vision (which of course inspires respect), you might think twice out walking through it, so retrace your steps and go left round the ▌. On the other side, if you push back a branch that marks the end of track, you emerge behind the same crosses, just as awesome. There is : another field of crosses higher up on the left.

This uniquely moving and disturbing place is known as the "little gels" graveyard. Despite what you might think, these aren't the graves unbaptised children (as in some countries), but children under the e of 7 whose parents had no means of paying for an official burial. No re bodies have been accepted since 2008.

TOMB OF
THE MARQUIS OF PARANÁ

Esoteric Egyptian tomb of a Carioca Freemason

Cemitério São João Batista
Rua General Polidoro
(21) 3217-3182 or (21) 3217-3183
saojoaobatista@riopax.com.br
Daily 7am–6pm
Free guided tours (booking required): cemiteriosjb.com.br/agendamento
Metro: Botafogo

Just to the left as you face the cemetery church, the hand of a fem
statue points to an inscription above the entrance to the esoteric b
ial chamber of the Marquis and Baron of Paraná.

A politician, diplomat and magistrate known for his conciliatory t
ents, Honório Hermeto Carneiro Leão, future Marquis of Paraná (180
1856), was above all a Freemason with a high degree in the Grand Ori
of Brazil Lodge. While still a student at the University of Coimbra, P
tugal, he had joined a secret society called A Gruta (The Den), found
by Brazilian students with the primary goal of changing Brazil fron
monarchy to a republi

The historic relatic
ship between Freem
sonry and the Egypti
tradition is evident he
the vault is shaped li
an Egyptian tem
and evokes the init
tory mysteries in whi
the three sides of t
pyramid express the
evation of the soul
heaven by invoking t
three Masonic tools
compass, set square a
sacred book.

The Marquis
Paraná lies here, en
balmed by Dr Peix
to, who followed t
Sucquet embalmi
method in the Egypti

dition, as requested by the deceased. The arrangement of the coffin is
so similar to the practice in ancient Egypt: the embalmed corpse was
aced in a sealed lead coffin, which was first placed in a varnished cedar
ffin. The second coffin was in turn placed inside another magnificent
ffin, donated by the brotherhood of the Santa Casa da Misericórdia do
o de Janeiro (Holy House of Mercy), which ran the necropolis. Three
ffins for one body, symbol of the three vital principles animating this
ortal coil: the mind, the psyche and the physical.

The female statue attired like an Egyptian priestess, who is facing the
mb and pointing to the inscription above the door, represents immor-
ity rather than death. This is shown by the Sun resplendent on her
rehead, a symbol of the god Ra, allegory of spiritual enlightenment, and
pecially the *ankh* crosses engraved on her robes with the letter A, initial
ankh (ancient Egyptian hieroglyph signifying "life"), representing the
nsciousness of immortality through Masonic initiation.

At the sides of the inscription are two hawks with acacia leaves in their
aks – the Masonic flower symbolises initiation and immortality and the
rds express the winged "soul" of the initiate, who returns to the eternal
rient having been absorbed by the Great Architect of the Universe.

The engravings of women playing the zither represent Nut, goddess
the Sky, wife of Geb (god of the Earth, protector of the dead), and
e the allegory of supreme wisdom suggested by the expressive music
universal harmony.

On the ledge above the door is the uraeus (serpent), the eye of Ho-
s, god of divine wisdom and spiritual kingship, indicated by the royal
rpents (Najas) surrounding the winged Sun. It is the Sun that trans-
its the vital fluid, the breath of life, which is why the ancient pharaohs
ore the rearing *uraeus* on their crowns. The royal serpents should be
terpreted as beings that repel evil and therefore protect the funerary
onuments and their occupants, reinforced by the presence of Horus,
n of Osiris and Isis (the Egyptian Trinity), which eternally fights the
rces of darkness for the victory of the forces of light, that is, for im-
ortality to succeed death.

Further protection is given by the sphinx opposite the female sta-
e, placed beside an entrance to the chamber to keep out strangers.
the passive position, the sphinx contemplating the single point on
e horizon where the Sun rises was considered the guardian of forbid-
n entrances and royal mummies. It is the representation of the divine
ysteries that surround death and survive the hazards of the cycles of
iman existence.

NEARBY

Stained-glass window commemorating the navy dead

Cemitério São João Batista is like an open-air museum – the headston range from eclectic to neo-Gothic and from Art Deco to neoclassic or modernist. In addition to individual and family graves, such as n mber 24013 belonging to composer Tom Jobim (1927–1994) or t

imposing tomb (133-E) the "father of aviatio Alberto Santos-Dumo (1873–1932), there are t impressive monuments the Acadêmia Brazileira Letras (section 29, 1778- and of the military auth rities. The tomb comm morating the Mortos Divisão Naval (behi vault 19970 in avenue is well worth a look. T work of sculptor Le Velloso (1899–1966), it h an Art Deco exterior an inside, a magnificent ab tract stained-glass windo and two statues with a m ditative air (see photo).

Chapel only open for Mass on Mondays and the Day of the Dead

At the far end of the main avenue is a chapel dating from the time of Dom Pedro II. This very simple little sanctuary only opens for Mass on Mondays at 9am and on the Dia de Finados (Day of the Dead, 2 November).

A Mass for the first burial in the cemetery was celebrated here on 4 December 1852, a few months after the land was acquired. It was for Rosaura, a slave girl aged 4, as none of the families of the local elite wished to "inaugurate" the cemetery.

Brazil's first abstract sculpture

Through the main entrance of São João Batista cemetery in Rua General Polidoro, to the left before the small office building, you'll discover what is considered to be the first abstract sculpture in Brazil.

This anthropomorphic statue with its very simple lines, made from a block of Carrara marble and bronze, represents geologist Orville Adelbert Derby (1851–1915).

This is probably the most important work in the cemetery, artistically speaking, because it dates from the early 20th century, at a time when other styles predominated.

The work is by the distinguished sculptor Rodolfo Bernardelli, who died in 1931 and was laid to rest in São João Batista's avenue 109-E, known as the "Vieira Souto" of the cemetery – an allusion to the sought-after beachside avenue of that name at Ipanema. Bernardelli himself requested that a beautiful neoclassical bronze sculpture he made in 1879 (when studying in Rome) should be placed on his tomb. It depicts the stoning of Stephen, the first Christian martyr.

Thanks to the many celebrities buried here, including nine former Presidents of the Republic, the cemetery has star quality. The money to purchase the land came from the sale of titles of nobility. Today, through new acquisitions, the total area of 183,000 m^2 has over 50,000 graves: Christians, other religions (there are more Jews buried here than in the Jewish cemetery at Vila Rosali) and atheists.

The most visited tomb is that of *música popular brasileira* singer Clara Nunes (1942–1983), who is venerated like a saint. People make offerings to her in thanks for pardons received.

PROJETO MORRINHO

Work of art in a favela

Pereirão favela
Visits available by appointment
You will be picked up at the entrance to the favela (access via Santa Teresa or
Laranjeiras)
Raniere Dias: (21) 96846 9527
Eder Freitas: (21) 98075 8127
or email ranetourguide@gmail.com

© Jean-Marc Joseph

n the Pereirão *favela* above Laranjeiras district, not far from Rio's French high school, the Morrinho ("small hill" in Portuguese, and y extension "small *favela*" in Rio) project is practically unknown to ariocas.

It has, however, been showcased around the world – at the 52nd enice Biennale in 2007 and at New York's MoMA in 2009, as well as ae Museu de Arte do Rio (MAR), which shows the project's trademark: niiniature reproductions of *favela* life, whose architecture, violence and pography intrigue the world.

It all started in 1997: Cilan Oliveira was 15 when he arrived in ereirão. To relieve his boredom, he reconstructed the streets and build- gs before his eyes with the materials to hand: bricks and earth.

The model grew so realistic that the police dealing with gang warfare ook the emerging work of art as a miniature plan of the *favela*. They uspected it was designed to plan drug or arms traffickers' escape routes uring military clean-up operations. The artists protested and eventual- convinced the authorities of their innocence, while their model nar- wly avoided destruction.

In 2002, two filmmakers lifted the project out of anonymity in a opular documentary. The international exhibitions held between 2004 ad 2009 came along like a fairy tale, with all the excesses of the art aarket.

Requests to show their work are fewer nowadays, although still regu- r, and the Morrinho project has expanded in four areas: film-making, ocial change projects, travelling exhibitions and tourism. As for Olivei- a: "I'll have succeeded when young people, after their experience here, an make a living from their art without our help."

The installation, which nowadays can be toured by calling in ad- ance, is constantly changing, just like the *favela* itself – monumental ad fragile at the same time, it has to be repaired after each rainstorm.

SOCIEDADE BUDISTA DO BRASIL

Buddhists in Santa Teresa

Estrada Dom Joaquim Mamede 45
(21) 2245-4331
sbb@sociedadebudistadobrasil.org
sociedadebudistadobrasil.org
Meditation every day except Sunday at 6pm
Sunday: meditation and teaching around 4.30pm–6.30pm
Thursday: study group 5pm
Option of silent spiritual retreats

You don't just stumble upon the site of the Buddhist Society of Brazil. And even in passing, it's easy to miss.

To find the centre, from Rua Almirante Alexandrino take Estrada Dom Joaquim Mamede, which connects Santa Teresa to the city centre, through Estrada do Sumaré. About 500 m further along on the left you'll see a flight of steps, covered with drawings and inscriptions announcing the site, leading to the forest. Leave the car and climb the hundred or so steps that lead to the centre itself. It was officially founded in 1967 by members of the Theosophical Society of Brazil.

The centre specialises in the teaching and practice of Theravāda, the oldest branch of Buddhism, practised mainly in Sri Lanka, Thailand, Myanmar, Cambodia and Laos.

It opens regularly for members and occasional visitors, offering meditation and teaching – an excellent opportunity to try meditation or learn more about Buddhism. Although strictly speaking there isn't a Buddhist monk running the centre or living there permanently, monks from around the world regularly stay for a few months.

The meditation sessions – there were around thirty participants during our visit – take place on the roof of a building, with a fine view of the neighbourhood.

Interestingly, the Cristo Redentor at Corcovado as seen from the meditation site seems to be blessing the centre, in a fine example of religious syncretism.

For some people, Jesus is indeed an avatar (manifestation) of the divine principle, as are Muhammad, Zoroaster, Buddha and Krishna.

ORMER VATICAN EMBASSY N RIO

palace directly inspired by the Palazzo Vecchio 1 Florence

entro Educacional Anísio Teixeira
ua Almirante Alexandrino 4098

The building at the corner of Rua Almirante Alexandrino and Rua Dom Joaquim Mamede looks like a Florentine palace. Dating from)42, the former Vatican Embassy is now occupied by the Centro Edu-.cional Anísio Teixeira (CEAT).

The banker Oscar Sant'Anna fell in love with the Palazzo Vecchio iring a trip to Italy and photographed it from every angle. Back in io, he asked architect Faro Filho to build him a palace inspired by his .ctures. The tower does indeed closely resemble that of its Florentine icestor (see photos).

The family then sold the palace to the Vatican. A chapel was added id the papal embassy established there until 1960, when the capital as moved from Rio to Brasilia. Note the papal arms on the stained-.ass window in the church.

Some of the house names in the alley just behind CEAT also evoke ; former owner: Villa Graças a Deus, Villa Santa Ephigenia, Villa S. abriel.

RUSSIAN ORTHODOX CHURCH OF ST ZINAIDA

From Russia to Rio

Rua Monte Alegre 210
(21) 2252-1471
Sunday around 9am–11.30am
Mass Sunday 10am

Not far from the Benjamin Constant House Museum, a little further down Rua Monte Alegre, onion-shaped golden domes attract the attention of curious passers-by. Santa Teresa's Russian Orthodox church, open only on Sunday mornings (just push open the door that looks closed), was built in 1927 by White Russians fleeing the Bolshevik Revolution. The Santa Teresa neighbourhood was chosen because many affluent Russians and Brazilians lived there: the district had prospered from 1850 because of its altitude, as yellow-fever carrying mosquitoes were much less of a problem.

Note that as in most Orthodox churches, you can't sit down and enjoy the atmosphere, the chanting and the iconostasis that separates the priest from the worshippers.

The church owes its name to the fact that the wife of the architect, Gleb Konstantinovich Sakharov, was called Zinaida. St Zinaida was a member of St Paul's family. The name means "of the family of Zeus" or "divine girl".

The first Russians arrived in Brazil in the late 19th century, mainly in Rio Grande do Sul, to cultivate the land.

NEARBY

The remains of the Santa Teresa cable car   ⑱

Museu Casa de Benjamin Constant
85 Rua Monte Alegre
(21) 3970-1177 / 3970-1168
Wednesday to Friday 1pm–5pm, weekends 10am–5pm

At the bottom left of the garden of the Benjamin Constant House Museum, you'll notice two circular holes in the wall. They were for the cables of the car that connected Rua de Matacavalos (old name for Rua Riachuelo) to the terminal at Largo do Guimarães, passing by the current museum.

Inaugurated in 1877, the cable car was operated by a steam engine until 1894, at the same time as the celebrated Santa Teresa tramway. Designed by engineer Jánurio Cândido de Oliveira, it extended over 1.3 m and three viaducts had to be constructed for it. The first station was at 89 Travessa do Castro.

FOUNDLINGS' WHEELS, CARMELITE CONVENTO DE SANTA TERESA

How to abandon your child discreetly

Ladeira de Santa Teresa 52 – Monday to Friday 6am–12pm and 2pm–5pm, Saturday and Sunday closes 4pm

Although there are several reproductions of foundlings' wheels in R (see opposite), those at Santa Teresa convent are the only ones st at their original site. These wooden wheels were used to abandon babi discreetly (see opposite). The two examples at the convent are in the sa risty, one to the right of the church, the other in the room to the left of t sanctuary, which also has some lovely azulejos. You'll see in both of the that the space at the bottom where you could leave your child is relative narrow, to stop older children being abandoned... The top part of the wheels was also used (and still is today) as a means of communication b tween the cloistered sisters and the rest of the world, without them havi to speak or be seen.

The first foundlings' wheel in Brazil was installed in El Salvador in 1726. In the second half of the 19th century, there were up to fourteen of them in the country. The last working example, removed in 1949, was in São Paulo. In Rio, they were in operation from 1738 for 200 years until abolished under legislation on minors in 1938.

A reproduction of a foundlings' wheel can be seen at the museum of the Brazilian Historical and Geographical Institute (see p. 115), another at the Brazilian Pediatrics Memorial Museum at Cosme Velho and a third at the Educandário (boarding school) Romão de Mattos Duarte (60 Rua Paulo VI, Flamengo), although the latter isn't on permanent display.

The House of the Wheel, later called the Foundlings' House and now Romão de Mattos Duarte boarding school in homage to its founder, was located next to the hospital of Santa Casa da Misericórdia, at Castelo, between 1738 and 1821. It moved several times, until settling at Flamengo in a large house built in 1911 on and that belonged to the Comte d'Eu, husband of Princess Isabel.

What is a foundlings' wheel?

It is said that in 787, Dateus, a priest in Milan, began placing a large basket outside his church so that abandoned infants could be left there. More organised initiatives for the reception of abandoned children were begun by the Hospice des Chanoines in Marseilles from 1188 onwards, with Pope Innocent III (1198-1216) later giving the practice the Church's benediction; he had been horrified by the terrible sight of the bodies of abandoned infants floating in the Tiber and was determined to do something to save them.

So the doors of convents were equipped with a sort of rotating cradle which made it possible for parents to leave their infant anonymously and without exposing it to the elements.

The infant was left in the outside section of the cradle, and then the parent rang a bell so that the nuns could activate the mechanism and bring the child inside. Access to the "turntable" was, however, protected by a grille so narrow that only newborn infants would fit through...

Abandoned during the 19th century, the system had to be readopted after some 20 years at various places in Europe due to the sharp upturn in the number of infants abandoned.

ACADEMIA BRASILEIRA DE LITERATURA DE CORDEL

Popular culture in academic rhymes

Rua Leopoldo Fróes 37
(21) 2232-4801 / 2221-1077
Daily 9am–5pm when Gonçalo isn't travelling

A short distance from Getulio Damaso's curious "tram-shape workshop where he recycles scrap materials, the Brazilian Aca my of Cordel Literature was founded by Gonçalo Ferreira da Silva. still runs it today.

The *cordel* – a booklet of "stories on a string" that has survived Brazil and Portugal as well as some other European countries – i collection of short texts in verse, intended to inform the non-read public who wouldn't buy an "expensive and time-consuming" book.

The *cordels* deal with many subjects: news items, recent and anci history, social phenomena, political analysis, economic, scientific or ographical – all the names that have left their mark on the world, fr Gandhi to Mao Zedong, Laplace to Archimedes.

Gonçalo Ferreira da Silva was born in 1937 in Ipu, in the state Ceara. His mother couldn't read at all, his father barely. He learr something of life through the kindness of neighbours but, havi known poverty, at the age of 14 he lied about his age to go to Rio Janeiro. After months of wandering and sleeping rough, he got to kn

e troubadours or *cordelistes*: he went to their meetings, where verbal
usting stimulated the search for a good rhyme, the right word, the
curacy of an idea. They all shared a deep knowledge of the Portu-
ese language. Gonçalo published his first booklet in 1978 and, with
other people, founded the academy on 7 September 1988. There are
rrently 40 of these lovers of their beautiful language, of wordplay and
od humour.

All of them bear in mind the motto *produzir, preservar, divulgar*
roduce, preserve, disclose). Their mission is limitless: offering modest
ople the opportunity to experience the world through the written
rd.

If you visit 37 Rua Leopoldo Fróes, you can buy a *cordel* (in several
nguages, for R$2 a copy) and chat with Gonçalo (in Portuguese). If
ch of his recitation of the legend of the *uirapuru* (the bird that sings
ly once a year and whose song commands total silence in the Amazon
est) is incomprehensible, don't worry: just savouring these rhymes
t bounce back and forth is still a great treat.

Where does the word "cordel" come from?

Cordel comes from the practice of offering the booklets hanging from
strings like washing in the wind, held up by clothes pegs. It was
a cheap way of displaying many copies in a small space. The illustrations in these booklets are monochrome woodcuts, engraved by
various artists in a simple but expressive style.

Copacabana – Urca

①	NAPOLEON'S LOCK OF HAIR	160
②	PAVEMENT DEDICATED TO CARLOS DRUMMOND DE ANDRADE	161
③	MOSAIC BY LYGIA CLARK	162
④	BIBLIOTECA ESCOLAR MUNICIPAL DE COPACABANA CARLOS DRUMMOND DE ANDRADE	163
⑤	IGREJA SANTA CRUZ DE COPACABANA	164
⑥	CHACRINHA STATE PARK	165
⑦	COPACABANA BATCAVE	166
⑧	REMAINS OF MORROS DO INHANGÁ	168
⑨	ITAHY BUILDING	170

10	ITAÓCA BUILDING	174
11	GUAHY BUILDING	176
12	LOBBY OF EDIFÍCIO PETRÔNIO	178
13	OBELISK TO MARK THE WIDENING OF AVENIDA ATLÂNTICA	180
14	MORRO DA BABILÔNIA HIKING TRAIL	182
15	STATUE OF CHOPIN	184
16	STAIRCASE AT THE MUSEU DE CIÊNCIAS DA TERRA	186
17	INSTITUTO CULTURAL CRAVO ALBIN	190
18	GUIDED TOUR OF FORTE DE SÃO JOSÉ	192

NAPOLEON'S LOCK OF HAIR

What's a lock of Napoleon's hair doing in Rio?

Museu Histórico do Exército
Forte de Copacabana
Praça Coronel Eugênio Franco 1 (end of Avenida Atlântica, posto VI)
fortedecopacabana.com
Tuesday to Sunday 10am–7pm
Metro: Praça General Osório
Bus: 121, 126, 127, 484, 455

W ho'd have imagined that a lock of the French Emperor's h
would be displayed in a Rio museum?

It's easy to miss in the "Gallery of Curiosities" of the Historical M
seum of the Army, despite sitting next to a small bust and statue
Napoleon Bonaparte.

This lock of hair was donated in 1992 by the family of Mars
Castelo Branco (first President of Brazil after the 1964 military co
d'état), after his death.

Although a short note in French in the glass case simply indica
that the lock was obtained after the Emperor died, the archives a
slightly more revealing.

Three weeks before his death, Napoleon dictated his will to his va
Marchand. Among other instructions, he wanted his hair cut off af
his death so that locks of it could be added to gold bracelets that were
be given to his mother and brothers.

Marchand respected Napoleon's instructions and cut his hair on t

occasions after his death. T
first time, he only cut the h
from the top of the skull and
body was displayed wearing
hat during the funeral ceremo
The rest of the hair was cut j
before burial.

We don't, however, kn
how many locks of hair w
taken, or how they were distr
uted beyond those stipulated
the will, or why Marshal Cast
Branco's family came into p
session of one of them.

AVEMENT DEDICATED TO ② CARLOS DRUMMOND DE ANDRADE

* amous poet next door*

rgo do Poeta
action of Avenida Rainha Elisabeth and Rua Conselheiro Lafaiete
etro: General Osório

At the junction of Avenida Rainha Elisabeth and Rua Conselhei-ro Lafaiete, known as Largo do Poeta (Poet's Plaza), it's easy to ss the Portuguese texts inscribed at the four corners of the pavement. ese are excerpts from four poems by Carlos Drummond de Andrade 902–1987), a leading Brazilian poet who lived nearby, at number 60 a Conselheiro Lafaiete:

vida futura nós te criaremos ("Oh future life we will create you" – from e poem *Mundo grande*)

agora José ("And now José" – *José*)

ntade de cantar mas tão absoluta que me calo repleto ("The will to sing t so absolute that I am silenced satisfied" – *Canto esponjoso*)

da história é remorso ("All history is remorse" – *Claro enigma*)

Largo do Poeta, Rio's posthu-ous tribute to the writer from inas Gerais, was inaugurated August 1990.

Andrade, a widely published et and journalist, was also ncipal private secretary to the inister of Education, Gustavo panema. The painting *Água* /ater), from the abstract series Cândido Portinari, hangs in office at the former minis-headquarters, now known as lácio Gustavo Capanema (see 46). Andrade loved to walk und the neighbourhood and gularly strolled down Avenida inha Elisabeth to the beach. ere, facing the ocean at Co-cabana, his famous bronze tue is seated on a bench along e promenade.

MOSAIC BY LYGIA CLARK

The first steps of a great artist

Avenida Atlântica 3392

At the entrance to the residential building at number 3992 Aveni
Atlântica, between Avenida Rainha Elisabeth and Rua Julio de C
tilhos, a genuine forgotten treasure of Brazilian contemporary art can
seen from the pavement: a multicoloured mosaic depicting the hum
body and various abstract shapes. The work mentions the year 1951 in
bottom right corner, beside the signature of Lygia Clark, one of Braz
most important artists. Art lovers will enjoy the challenge of trying
identify, in this work by someone who was in the process of becoming
painter and sculptor, the early stages of the body of great work produc
by Lygia Clark. A revolutionary artist who described herself as a "non-a
ist", Clark destroyed paradigms and broke away from the limits of forr
art. In 1954, for example, she was already incorporating the frame in
her works as a physical element.

Lygia Clark, one of the founders of Neoconcretism, was born in Be
Horizonte in the state of Minas Gerais in 1920 and died in Rio de Jane
in 1988. She moved gradually from two- to three-dimensional art and
1960 created the *Bichos*, structures made from metal sheets, which inv
the observer to handle them. She subsequently continued to explore t
senses, investigated bodily experiences and concentrated on the therape
tic possibilities of sensory art. This all led her, towards the end of her li
to see her work as being closer to psychoanalysis. Clark's work has receiv
international recognition and major museums throughout the world ha
held retrospectives devoted to her. Her work achieved record sums fo
Brazilian artist in 2013 in auctions held in Brazil and abroad.

> Such is the importance of the *Bichos* in Lygia Clark's work that in
> 2015, to celebrate the 95th anniversary of her birth, Google paid
> homage to her with a special Doodle depicting the *Bichos*.

To live happily, live hidden

Long-standing residents of the street who use the library today
claim that the house has no windows because the owner didn't
want passersby to see the goings-on inside. The remains of the wall
in the little garden next to the street seem to confirm this version
of events: in other words, the master of the house asked for a flight
of steps leading directly to his bedroom so he could conduct his
amorous liaisons discreetly.

IBLIOTECA ESCOLAR MUNICIPAL ④ E COPACABANA CARLOS RUMMOND DE ANDRADE

he house with no windows

a Sá Ferreira 80 – Metro: Praça General Osório (Sá Ferreira exit)
) 2267-5561 / 2227-0783
nday to Friday 9am–5pm, last entry 4.45pm (admission free)

*W*edged in beside Rua Saint Roman, a steep street leading to the Cantagalo-Pavão-Pavãozinho group of favelas, the Copacabana unicipal School Library is located in one of the city's most unusual ildings. Thanks to its Art Deco details and overlapping volumes, this is nsidered the most advanced Brazilian architectural project of the 1920s.

Although the small library, popularly known as "the house with no ndows", is meant for children (who call it the "witch's castle"), it wel-mes grown-ups as well.

The building, which was listed by the city of Rio in 1996, is officially own as Casa Villiot. Designed by the Italian architect Antonio Virzi e p. 125), it was the residence of engineer Victor Villiot Martins. When e house was built in 1929, it made such an impression that the Presi-nt of the Brazilian Republic himself, Washington Luís, paid a visit. This Virzi's last-known work in Rio.

Half-hidden behind a wall, the house almost waits to be discovered by ssers-by. But once inside, its beauty and inventiveness are immediately parent: despite the lack of windows, pleasant natural light filters through any small coloured-glass panels and e two fountains (out of order) in at were once the living and dining oms.

This two-storey residence was re-ored in 2006. Although the shelves books make it difficult to see certain tails and interior perspectives, you n still appreciate the corners, curves, gles and decorative hand-painted nels, as well as the superb original np fittings. Also look out for the th, on the second floor near the for-er bedroom.

IGREJA SANTA CRUZ DE COPACABANA

A modern church on a shopping-centre terrace

Shopping Cidade Copacabana (also known as Shopping dos Antiquários or Antiques Mall)
Rua Siqueira Campos 143, 4th floor
(21) 2235-3200
Daily
Admission free
Metro: Siqueira Campos

The small church of Santa Cruz de Copacabana is hidden away on sort of wide concrete terrace dotted with a few potted plants, a fe metres from the metro station between Siqueira Campos and Figueire Magalhães streets.

Take the little-used circular ramps in Cidade Copacabana shoppi centre as far as the fourth and last floor to find it. The 400 m² church h glass walls, and the gently curving concrete roof takes the form of tw merging vaults. This gives a feeling of lightness, in contrast to the gr mass of the surrounding buildings.

This church with its pared-down decoration was consecrated in J 1961 even before the construction of the mall was completed. Ap from its modernist architecture, it is also worth a visit to see the faith replica of the Turin Shroud (a length of linen purporting to be the bur garment of Christ) on the wall behind the altar.

This silk-screen print w donated to the church in t early 2000s by the Italian Si donology Centre (Shro Studies).

The Cidade Copacaba centre, designed by archite Mindlin & Associados, was o of the first in Rio de Janeiro.

It features long corrid and a spiral ramp reminisce of the one in New York's Gu genheim Museum, very bo for its time, which smooth the flow of visitors.

CHACRINHA STATE PARK   ⑥

Copacabana's hidden park

End of Rua Guimarães Natal, between Ladeira do Leme and Rua Assis
Brasil
Tuesday to Sunday 8am–5pm
Metro: Cardeal Arcoverde

Strolling through the noisy Rua Barata Ribeiro, the location of Cardeal Arcoverde metro station, you'd never guess that at the end of Rua Guimarães Natal is the entrance to Chacrinha State Park, amid the buildings and hills of São João and Babilônia. This park, one of the last areas with traces of the Atlantic forest in the Zona Sul, has a hiking trail that can be covered in about an hour.

Besides the plant and animal life, the remaining traces throw light on aspects of the history of the neighbourhood and of Rio. In particular, at the end of the path, you'll discover the ruined foundations of the Casa de Teodoro (Teodoro's House). Probably dating from the early 19th century, it was built of stone, clay and shells. It is said to be the oldest residence in Copacabana and is thought to have belonged to a fisherman called Teodoro.

Some of the park's paths were originally trodden by the indigenous people and by the soldiers protecting the city. The "mule path", for example, was opened during the colonial period to transport provisions for the soldiers guarding Rio.

You can also see the ruins of the lookout platforms, a shrine, and the aqueduct that carried water collected on the rocky slopes of the hill to a fountain, whose remains are still visible.

Near the entrance to the park (which covers 13.3 hectares) is a recreation and sports area. Some climbers also venture off the historical-natural path.

Although formally established in 1969 as the first city park, it was only about 20 years later that Chacrinha began to fulfil its role of public space and to assume its nature preservation mission.

Until then, it was occupied by *favela*, used as landfill and for a samba school.

COPACABANA BATCAVE

Batman in Rio

Cardeal Arcoverde metro station
Rua Barata Ribeiro, by Rua Rodolfo Dantas
Daily during metro operating hours

tep onto a platform of Cardeal Arcoverde metro station and you'll
think you're in a cave – much of the walls and ceiling seem to be
re rock with a rough cement coating.

The same design is found in the corridors on the floor above, where
e station's long ventilation shaft rises to the surface. If you stand under
e duct and have a good look upwards, however, the legendary Batman
go is lit up.

This unexpected sight is one more example of Carioca humour and
everence. It all started shortly before the station opened, when an
gineer brought his children to see the construction work, joking that
is was Batman's cave.

The children were excited to hear that but insisted on proof. So
e of the engineers thought of attaching the Batman logo to the duct
tlet.

On their next visit, the children were thrilled: that was what had
en missing to confirm Batcave status! After the station opened in June
98, passengers also grew fond of the local Batman.

So much so, according to older employees, that when the logo faded
vay, the public demanded a replacement. The current logo is the third.

A station with dozens of copies of Brazilian rocks

In the station garden on Rua Barata Ribeiro, a large pink boulder
sets the scene for what lies inside.

Unlike all Rio's other stations, the floor here is covered with dozens
of samples of Brazilian rocks, "formed over 400 million years ago",
according to the engraving on a steel door half hidden on the Zona
Norte platform.

Entitled *Embarque na Estação Terra* (Boarding at Earth Station),
the text explains the formation of the planet and describes the
rocks in these words: "Time and the movements of the Earth are
the artists that created the rocks. The inks they used are mixtures of
molecules and atoms."

REMAINS OF MORROS
DO INHANGÁ

The flight of steps that divides the avenue in two

Avenida Nossa Senhora de Copacabana, next to number 374
Metro: Cardeal Arcoverde

Between 374 Avenida Nossa Senhora de Copacabana and Sala Bad-
Powell is a long flight of 75 steps; they follow the remains of t-
former Morros do Inhangá, which divided Avenida Nossa Senhora -
Copacabana. The steps end at Rua General Barbosa Lima, a reside-
tial street of apartments and houses. Rua General Azevedo Pimentel-

iet little street that is actually a dead end, runs from the other side of
e *morro* to Avenida Barata Ribeiro, opposite Praça Cardeal Arcoverde.
ere is another flight of 77 steps leading to the top of the hill. The walk
ves you an idea of the transformation Copacabana has undergone.

Until the 1920s, one of the three *morros* was behind one side of
e famous Copacabana Palace Hotel. The hill was excavated to build
venida Nossa Senhora de Copacabana, then divided, to become one
ng boulevard of 3.2 km. In 1934, another little hill was wiped off the
ap to construct the pool at Copacabana Palace (until Avenida Atlân-
ca was opened in 1906,
is hill cut the beach in
o at high tide).

Whatever still re-
ained in 1951 was de-
olished to make way
r the Chopin, Balada
d Prelúdio buildings
ext to the hotel.

There are also remains of this last section of the *morro* behind the
buildings between Rua Fernando Mendes and Rua Republica do
Peru. You can gather some idea of how it used to look from the
patio of Pedro Alvares Cabral college.

Inhangá comes from *Anhangá*, a word of Tupí-Guaraní origin meaning "evil spirit", "wandering soul" or "spirit that wanders". The
name seems to have come about because the rocky slopes of the
morro attracted lightning during storms.

Copacabana Palace Hotel, listed as national heritage, was built to
receive visitors to the International Exposition celebrating the centenary of Brazilian independence from Portugal in 1922 (see p. 52).
However, it only opened in 1923 due to contractors' delays and
violent storm damage to the lower floors in 1922. Despite none
of the scenes being filmed there, the hotel inspired the Hollywood
musical *Flying Down to Rio*, when Fred Astaire and Ginger Rogers
danced together for the first time. The whole thing was shot in
Hollywood studio sets reproducing parts of the hotel.

ITAHY BUILDING

The symbol of Art Deco native to Rio

Avenida Nossa Senhora de Copacabana 252
Metro: Cardeal Arcoverde

f there is one Rio building that symbolises local Art Deco and represents the indigenous influence on Brazilian Modernismo, it has to be
ne Itahy, at 252 Avenida Nossa Senhora de Copacabana.

The building was designed in 1932 by Arnaldo Gladosch. This São
aulo architect, the son of German immigrants, trained in Europe in
926 at the Königlich-Sächsisches Polytechnikum (Royal Saxon Pol-
echnic Institute). The Itahy blends different references, its entrance
pped by a spectacular "Indian-mermaid-caryatid" and the sleek aer-
dynamic lines of refined Art Deco architecture in the body of the
uilding.

Pedro Correia de Araújo, who was responsible for the decoration of
ne portico and lobby, was born in Paris and lived there until the 1920s.
le came from a noble family from Pernambuco (old and trusted friends
f Emperor Dom Pedro II, who emigrated to Paris with him when he
ent into exile after the proclamation of the Republic in 1889). Correia
e Araújo knew Picasso, Léger and Matisse, among others, while he was
: the Académie Ranson (an art school founded by French painter Paul
anson).

Correia de Araújo returned to Brazil with nativist ideas, influenced
y artist Ivan da Silva Bruhns, another Brazilian living in Paris and one
f the most important exponents of the art of tapestry. Seeing Brazil
om afar let them appreciate how an individual style could spring from
neir own background.

The cylindrical ceramic pieces that frame the entrance to the building
now the influence of the Printemps department store's design studio at
ne 1925 International Exposition of Modern Decorative and Industrial
rts in Paris. The entrance door of hammered metal is ornamented with
nages of seaweed and turtles. Inside the hall, a tiled floor features ocean
aves. The walls have relief carvings of fish and other marine symbols.

In the neighbouring district of Leme, Rua Gustavo Sampaio, the
Manguaba building also features decorative art by Pedro Correia de
Araújo. Similar aerodynamic architecture (by Chaves & Campelo,
1936) highlights the marriage between nativism and modernism.
Ceramic panels at the entrance, majolica columns... all lead back
to the Itahy.

Rio de Janeiro, capital of Latin America Art Deco

The city of Rio de Janeiro has over 400 significant Art Deco buildings, including the largest monument of its kind, the Cristo Redentor (Christ the Redeemer) at Corcovado. At least 200 of these would be worthy of inclusion in any collection dedicated to the movement.

Carioca Art Deco developed over the period 1920 to 1950. Its heyday coincided with the government of Getúlio Vargas, in particular during the dictatorship of the Estado Novo (New State) from 1937 to 1945. Vargas wanted to show Rio de Janeiro to the world as the symbol of a new Brazil, a showcase of modernity and global potential, and the universal architectural language of 1930s avant-garde was Art Deco.

Some government buildings of the time, like those of the Ministries of War, Labour and Finance, are icons of the genre.

The majority of official buildings – post offices, airports, the Central do Brasil railway station (along with the Ministry of War, the station forms the largest Art Deco district in Latin America), state schools – adopted the Art Deco style, both in its historical references and its streamlined aerodynamics.

Whereas in Europe, the First and Second World Wars had made all tourism impossible between 1914 and 1918 and 1939 and 1945 (respectively, the gestation period and apogee of Art Deco), Rio de Janeiro had become an ideal tourist destination. And much more: European stocks of Art Deco objects, furniture, artworks in general, were widely collected in South America. Brazilian ships left home with the raw materials for war or essentials such as iron, rubber, chocolate and coffee, and returned from Europe laden with crystal, porcelain and bronzes...

If we had to date the high point of Carioca Art Deco, we'd highlight the two cruises to the Rio Carnaval in 1938 and 1939 of the French transatlantic liner *Normandie* (the largest, most modern and luxurious of its time), organised by Boston agent Raymond Whitcomb. During the North Atlantic winter, there were no passengers on the *Normandie*'s usual route (Le Havre–Southampton–New York). Seizing the opportunity, Whitcomb hired the liner and managed to fully book it right away. Some of the Art Deco cabins, of various designs, cost the equivalent of US$130,000.

On arrival at Guanabara, the immense size of the *Normandie* meant that it had to anchor in Botafogo Bay rather than tie up in port. The liner was transformed into a real spectacle, lit up at night and open to the public by day. Visitor tickets could be purchased at the office of the Compagnie Générale Transatlantique.

Today, Rio de Janeiro is the undisputed Art Deco capital of Latin America: in 1996, at the first international seminar of Art Deco in Latin America, more than 500 participants paid tribute to this cultural heritage. In 2011, the 11th World Congress on Art Deco was organised in Rio by the International Coalition of Art Deco Societies (ICADS) and Brazil's Art Deco Institute (the pioneering society founded in 2005) – the first time the congress had been held in a Latin American country.

ITAÓCA BUILDING

An Art Deco amulet?

Rua Duvivier 43
Metro: Cardeal Arcoverde

One of the first buildings of over ten storeys in Copacabana – Itaóc at 43 Rua Duvivier – has brought a sophisticated European fla to the neighbourhood. With staff rooms on the top floor, it is for bo commercial and residential use, notably the street-level apartments th are the headquarters of the Alliance Française.

Designed in 1928 by architects Anton Floderer and Robert Prenti and built by the Christiano & Nielsen company, the building has

reamlined feel with projecting volumes, rounded corners and hori-
ntal friezes, and a nativist-inspired entrance with striking columns of
een majolica.

On these columns, as in the main section of the building, there are
ements which reference the Amazonian amulets know as *muiraquitãs*
ee below). Perhaps designed by Fernando Correia Dias, the nativist
egories of Itaóca have yet to be investigated. There is, however, no
ubt about the building's front door: it comes from the same factory as
at of the neighbour-
g Itahy building (see
170).

side, flooring with al-
rnating green and yel-
w lozenges evokes the
azilian flag. A large
terior patio (unusual
r Copacabana) sup-
ies the building with
ntilation and lighting.

Muiraquitãs: *Amazonian amulets*

The *muiraquitã* is an amulet to which indigenous tribes, mainly
Amazonian, attribute magical powers. These amulets might be
stone, clay, ceramic or even wood. They take the form of animals such as frogs (as in the entrance to the Itaóca building) or
alligators, but also stylised human figures. In Mário de Andrade's
novel *Macunaíma* (1928), hailed as the nativist epic of Brazilian
Modernismo, the plot develops around the search for a lost
muiraquitã.
In July 1925, at the Théâtre des Champs-Élysées in Paris, the ballet
"Legends, Beliefs and Amulets of the Amazon Indians" – adapted by
P.L. Duchartre from images drawn by Brazilian modernist Vicente
do Rego Monteiro – was performed to great acclaim. For fifteen
days, while the International Exposition of Modern Decorative and
Industrial Arts (a World's Fair dedicated to Art Deco) was held in
the city, attracting visitors from around the world, the theatre on
Avenue Montaigne was always packed.
In Brazil, sculptor Victor Brecheret incorporated Amazonian *mui-
raquitãs* into various works in bronze, terracotta or marble.

GUAHY BUILDING

One of Rio's most significant Art Deco buildings

Rua Ronald de Carvalho 181
Metro: Cardeal Arcoverde

he Guahy building, a Ricardo Buffa project dating from 1932, is one of the most important Art Deco buildings in Rua Ronald de arvalho and the Copacabana district.

Guahy, rooted in the "Cubist House" project (see photo) of Ray-ond Duchamp-Villon (1876–1918), was presented at the Paris Salon Automne in 1912 but was never carried through.

If only by its shape, the building also highlights the nativist in-ences of modern architects: the lines of the balcony railings and the ain doorway recall the decorative arts of the Marajoara (indigenous bes of the Ilha de Marajó, an island near Belém in northern Brazil) d the entrance gate represents their traditional headgear. Not to men-on the name Guahy, also of indigenous origin.

Guahy was threatened with demolition in the 1980s after it was pur-ased by an investor from Minas Gerais who was planning to open hotel on the site. Thanks to the intervention of Luiz Paulo Conde, anning administrator of Rio de Janeiro at the time, the building was otected and listed, and the purchaser was obliged to restore it instead knocking it down. Around this period, the process began of preser-ng the entire Lido district of Copacabana, which has about 50 Art eco buildings worth restoring and preserving.

Many TV productions, including the Globo network *telenovelas* aps), were filmed here, either on site or in studio sets.

Ricardo Buffa is also the architect of one of the most interesting Carioca buildings at 108 Rua Hermenegildo in Barros (Santa Teresa). The entrance is surrounded by Art Deco pillars.

Poet, writer and art critic, Ronald de Carvalho, after whom the street is named, was one of the mentors of Brazilian Modernismo.

Roxy staircase copies ocean liner

The beautiful Art Deco staircase of the Roxy cinema (945A Avenida Nossa Senhora de Copacabana), designed in 1934 by Brazilian ar-chitect Raphael Galvão, is a faithful copy of the one in the dining room of *The Atlantic*, an ocean liner that entered into service in 1930.

LOBBY OF EDIFÍCIO PETRÔNIO

*A building inspired by a project of Adolf Loos for
Josephine Baker*

Rua Ronald de Carvalho 45
Metro: Cardeal Arcoverde

Also known as Edifício Almeida Magalhães, the Petrônio buildin
was designed in 1934 by Carlos Porto and Caio Moacyr for th
entrepreneur owner Petrônio de Almeida Magalhaes.

This is one of the most remarkable buildings in Copacabana: a
though its facade echoes the aerodynamic streamlining of its neighbo
(see opposite), the entrance offers superb colour contrasts, using Eur
pean marbles (Siena yellow and Portoro black) on the walls, the flo
and the central column.

These bands of colour are thought to have been inspired by a 192

oject by Austrian architect Adolf Loos (author of the 1908 man-
sto *Ornament and Crime*, attacking ornamentation in art), for the
me of Josephine Baker, Franco-American muse of Art Deco. Never
ilt – though the plans have been reproduced in various books and
hibitions – the house was meant to be completely covered with black
d white stripes, in an obvious reference to the artist's roots and the
hite" world of her devoted fans. Baker visited Rio de Janeiro for the
st time in 1929 and received a standing ovation at the Cassino Beira
ar theatre.

Copacabana's first skyscraper

The nearby OK building (1928) at the corner of Rua Ronald de
Carvalho and Avenida Atlântica, now known as the Ribeiro Moreira
building, is considered to be the first skyscraper in Copacabana
with its fourteen floors.

OBELISK TO MARK THE WIDENING OF AVENIDA ATLÂNTICA

A souvenir of 1910 Copacabana

Praça Júlio de Noronha
Metro: Cardeal Arcoverde

In the farthest reaches of the Leme neighbourhood, a small obelisk Praça Júlio de Noronha is hardly ever noticed, yet it commemorat an important fact of Carioca life: the widening of Avenida Atlântica 12 m in 1910.

Up to that time, the avenue was still quite small: one lane in each direction, two sidewalks, and a central reservation with a few street lights installed together with the obelisk that is now at Leme.

In the 1930s, the central reservation was eliminated and the obelisk, which had stood on Rua Almirante Gonçalves, was transferred to its current location. Unfortunately, it has suffered from vandalism: much of the bronze lettering has disappeared, making it almost impossible to read the inscription.

The avenue only took on its current appearance in the 1970s: under the engineer Hildebrando de Góes Filho, the beach itself was significantly extended and again the avenue was widened. Roberto Burle Marx was commissioned to design the famous waves on the sidewalk (incidentally, he changed the initial direction of the waves to the design we know today).

Although the avenue, with its six lanes, is useful for drivers, it's a nightmare for others: local residents (who can't open their windows because of the deafening noise) or those who'd like a drink at one of the beach bars (it's sometimes difficult to hear your neighbour), not to mention the disappointing quality of the bars and restaurants because of lack of space. Just suppose that, with improved public transport, the avenue could rediscover a human scale (two lanes instead of the current six?). The space gained from the roadway could finally be used to create bars and restaurants worthy of the name, where you would listen to conversations and waves instead of the endless buses and their exhaust fumes, just like at the bars along the Arpoador peninsula...

MORRO DA BABILÔNIA HIKING TRAIL

A fantastic and little-known trail

Favela Inn – Rua Dr Nelson 32
Chapéu Mangueira–Leme
(21) 3209-2870 / 99568-4966
Admission: R$30 to R$40
Bus: 535, 538, 472, 190

The little-known trail in the Environmental Protection Area (APA, Área de Proteção Ambiental) of Morro da Babilônia (Babylon hill) overlooking the *favelas* of Babilônia and Chapéu Mangueira, makes outstanding walk. From its 200 m peak, the steep ridge offers som magnificent and unusual views of the city: from Corcovado to Sugarlo Mountain, from Copacabana to Pedra da Gávea, from Botafogo B and Aterro ("landfill") do Flamengo to Centro and the Zona Norte.

The local residents, organised into cooperatives, have reforested t area and they maintain the trails. The walk takes about three hou For the start of the itinerary, make your way through the busy stree of Babilônia.

The guide, born and raised in the *favela*, shows you the results recent reurbanisation: the contrast between the "new", with its exclusi ews of the world-famous sands of Praia de Copacabana, and the rustic, most rural, areas.

Shortly after passing the last houses along the way, you'll go back in me to discover the home of Seu Antônio. This mud hut, where he has ved for 71 years, was built by his grandfather in 1902. It offers a strik-g contrast to today's solidly built housing with its running water and nitation. Seu Antônio, in his friendly way, might well invite you in.

The most significant species of local fauna and flora are identified on ards set along the trail (in English and Portuguese). There are also the ins of the city's defence system from the colonial era and the Second Vorld War.

Since 2009 and the installation of a Police Pacification Unit (UPP – nidade de Polícia Pacificadora), the *favelas* of Babilônia and Chapéu langueira have seen many changes, not always controversy-free, inclung urban planning schemes and local micro-business initiatives.

Morro de Babilônia at Cannes

Orfeu Negro (*Black Orpheus*), winner of the 1959 Cannes Film Festival Palme d'Or and an Oscar for Best Foreign Film in 1960, transposes the tragic love story of Orpheus and Eurydice to a Rio *favela* during Carnaval. The score by Tom Jobim and Vinicius de Moraes is one of the references for bossa nova (new beat). The opening and closing scenes with the dying Orpheus and Eurydice, among others, were shot in Pedra do Urubu, near the top of Babylon hill.

Although the Leme neighbourhood was established in 1894, around the same time as Ipanema, Chapéu Mangueira dates from 1889, with shacks that were built at the site of the present-day Forte de Leme. In Rua General Ribeiro da Costa stood the house and first workshop (no longer there) of landscaper Roberto Burle Marx (1909–1994). Strolling up the steep streets of the *favela* to Rua Barroso, you'll also discover the large yellow residence that belonged to the celebrated Brazilian composer Ary Barroso (1903–1964). Among other popular songs, he wrote *Aquarela do Brasil*. The former community leader Benedita da Silva, who was elected councillor, then governor of Rio de Janeiro *estado* (state), also lived in Chapéu Mangueira. Apart from *Orfeu Negro*, other movies and TV soap opera scenes have been filmed in the community, including *Babilônia 2000*, directed by Eduardo Coutinho.

STATUE OF CHOPIN

Chopin confiscated

Praia Vermelha
Bus 107, 167, 513, 518, 519

uring the Nazi invasion of Poland in 1939, Polish radio insistently broadcast Chopin's *Polonaise* (Opus 40) to keep up the people's pariotic spirit. This is why the Germans, when they took over the country, destroyed the composer's statue in Warsaw. In response, Polish expatriates in Rio commissioned a statue of Chopin from August Zamoysky, who lived in the city from 1938 to 1955. The statue was delivered in 1944 and installed in Praça General Tibúrcio, in Urca. In 1951 the mayor of Rio, Mendes de Morais, asked for it to be moved in front of the Teatro Municipal (see opposite) but at every Carnaval, Chopin found himself decorated with garlands, confetti and various musical instruments.

In 1960, baritone Paulo Fortes wanted to protest at the 19th-century operatic composer Carlos Gomes being forgotten. Fortes raised funds to release the maquette for the statue that Rodolfo Bernardelli had made for the city of Campinas (Gomes' birthplace) from the National School of Fine Arts. He had a new statue cast in a foundry on Rua Camerino, recruited four removal men and, in the morning, "confiscated" the Chopin statue. After lying forgotten for a while in a warehouse, the sculpture was finally restored to Praia Vermelha in 1964. In its place, in front of the Municipal Theatre, Fortes installed the statue of the greatest composer of the Americas, Carlos Gomes. It has recently been moved round the side of the theatre.

Why was Chopin's statue placed in front of the Municipal Theatre in 1951?

The sculpture *Mulher com ânfora* (*Woman with Amphora*) by Humberto Cozzo used to stand in Praça Floriano (Cinelândia) in the early 1930s. It was designed to embellish (and conceal) the small water tower built to supply the theatre during renovations. The work was coordinated by engineer Doyle Maia under the leadership of the then mayor Pedro Ernesto, administrator of the federal district between 1931 and 1936. The base of the statue features two medallions: on one side, Pedro Ernesto, who had commissioned the work to restore the theatre and, on the other, Pereira Passos, who had originally built it.

According to Brazilian historian Raimundo Magalhães Júnior, mayor Mendes de Morais wanted to remove the figure of his predecessor Ernesto from the Cinelândia district, so he replaced Cozzo's sculpture with the Chopin statue. *Mulher com ânfora* was moved to Glória, then again in front of Candelária church, where it still stands.

STAIRCASE AT THE MUSEU DE CIÊNCIAS DA TERRA

A dramatic forgotten staircase

Avenida Pasteur and praça General Tibúrcio 404
(21) 2546-0257
mcter@sgb.gov.br
Tuesday to Saturday 10am–4pm
Admission free
Bus: 107, 511, 512 and 513

The Museum of Earth Sciences is the last vestige of the Exposição Nacional held in 1908 to celebrate the centenary of the opening of the ports (see following double-page spread). It has a rich collection of minerals and a few rooms dedicated to palaeontology and geology, in a quaint but charming setting.

There is a particularly striking staircase leading to beautiful offices (not open to the public). The three paintings on the stairs (allegories of trade, industry and agriculture) are the work of painter Antônio Pariras Niterói (1860–1937), who received a gold medal at the Seville World's Fair (Expo 29) in 1929.

The building, designed in 1880 by engineer Paula Freitas to house the faculty of the University of Medicine Pedro II, was left unfinished, and work only resumed on the occasion of the National Exposition of 1908. The neoclassical building, formerly the Palácio dos Estados (States Palace), was the main pavilion. It covered 7,600 m² and had ninety-one rooms. The building was occupied successively by the Ministry of Agriculture, the Veterinary School of Agronomy and the National Department of Mineral Production.

Other than the National Exposition, the statues in front of the former Hotel Glória are another relic of the anniversary celebrations of the opening of the ports in 1808.

The 1908 Exposição Nacional: from "pestilential" to "marvellous" city

Between 1903 and 1906, under prefect Pereira Passos (1836–1913), Rio saw extensive urbanisation schemes to modernise the city, eliminate epidemics and reduce the number of deaths caused by its generally insalubrious conditions. The ambience had been enough to earn Rio the nickname "pestilential city".

As urban renewal was changing the face of the Federal capital, a National Exposition was organised in 1908 to present this "new" city and the country's greater integration in an increasingly metropolitan and cosmopolitan world (Brazil participated in six World's Fairs between 1862 and 1904). The date was chosen to mark the centenary of the opening of Brazil's ports to friendly nations.

In his inauguration speech, President Afonso Pena (1847–1909) stated that the exhibition was intended to "make an inventory of the country", presenting its natural resources, production capacity and economic development.

The city's advanced public services were also highlighted – in particular, statistics showing that yellow fever had been eradicated the previous year and that fewer people would now die of smallpox and bubonic plague in the Federal District.

The 1908 Exposition was held between Saudade (now the site of Rio Yacht Club) and Vermelha beaches in the Urca neighbourhood from August to November. It was a hugely successful event: a million paying visitors passed through, whereas the city had only around 800,000 residents.

With over thirty pavilions, it surpassed the size of the London, Sydney and Melbourne Expos. The only pavilion that still survives is the States Pavilion, which stood not far from the monumental gates. Today it is the Museum of Earth Sciences (see p. 186), a theme related to the main focus of the Exposition.

At the far end of this axis stood the Industries Pavilion, in the former military academy.

The academy had been renovated using the newly invented material, reinforced concrete. It had its own light source and imposing fountains, forming what was called the *château d'eau* (French for "water tower").

The academy was demolished in 1938 to make way for the vast Praça General Tibúrcio.

Apart from its use of new materials, the Exposition facilities also served as a showcase for infrastructure solutions and urban

development: a wharf was built on Saudade beach to accommodate the boats coming from the Pharoux docks (now Praça XV), a
tramway was opened on Botafogo beach, and a small train carried
visitors between pavilions.

Origin of the expression "Cidade maravilhosa"

It was the writer and politician Coelho Neto (1864–1934) who in
1908, inspired by the new face of the city at the time, coined the
nickname that defined Rio as the "marvellous city".
For more information on why the ports were opened in 1808, and
what this meant, see p. 123.

INSTITUTO CULTURAL CRAVO ALBIN

Little-known musical treasures

Avenida São Sebastião 2
(21) 2295-2532
institutocravoalbin.com.br
Monday to Friday 1pm–5pm (visits on reservation only)
Admission free
Bus: 107, 511, 512, 513 (connection with metro at Botafago station)

1 the modest building at the top of Avenida São Sebastião, nobody would guess that the narrow elevator leading to the fourth floor opens to an area of around 3,000 m^2 spread over three levels, with many hall rooms, a terrace and an amazing garden with spectacular views er Botafogo Bay below Sugarloaf Mountain.

This is the home of the little–known Cravo Albin Cultural Institute, non-profit organisation set up in late 2001 to promote Brazilian culre and especially its music. The institute has a notable collection of ,000 disks (LPs, 78s and compacts) and about 5,000 CDs, reference deo and music programmes, sheet music and photographs.

In an atmosphere reminiscent of a family home, filled with ancestral emories, a mini-museum displays instruments and costumes of Braian music personalities, pictures and craft objects.

On the fourth and fifth floors, beyond the rooms reserved for the usic collection, is the reproduction of a 1930s/40s radio station with e microphone used by Carmen Miranda on Radio Mayrink Veiga. u can also see (and touch) Luiz Gonzaga's accordion, Cartola's guitar d the hats of Tom Jobim and Pixinguinha. There's also a collection of dios from different eras.

From the fifth-floor terrace you can enjoy panoramic views of Praia Urca and the iconic former casino (Cassino da Urca), now the Intuto Europeu do Design. Follow the walkway and concrete steps at e far end for a surprise: a garden with belvedere and small oval pool nding among the rocks of Morro da Urca. There, in 1962, among e profusion of plant life, the building used for the institute's cultural ents and temporary exhibitions was built out of recuperated materi-s. The facade is a replica of the home of Bishop José Castelo Branco's other, Ana Teodoro, who lived between 1731 and 1805 at Cinelândia a house that is now the *Biblioteca Nacional* (National Library).

The area in front of her house was known as *Largo da Mãe do Bispo* quare of the Bishop's Mother), the name inscribed on a plaque in the rden as a tribute to this influential figure of colonial Rio.

GUIDED TOUR OF FORTE DE SÃO JOSÉ

Birthplace of the city, unprecedented views, Art Deco gym...

Avenida João Luiz Alves
(21) 2543-3323 / 2586-2291
Saturday and Sunday 10am–1.30pm (duration two hours)
Reservations: sitiohistorico.fsj@gmail.com

Book by e-mail (address above) and you can visit the remarkable si of the military fort of São José, deep in the Urca neighbourhoo just beyond the famous Urca bar.

The guided tour, which lasts two hours, begins with the sports m seum (where various sporting artefacts of rather limited interest are di played) before heading to the fort itself on Morro Cara de Cao – th opportunity for a very pleasant walk of around 15 minutes, offerin

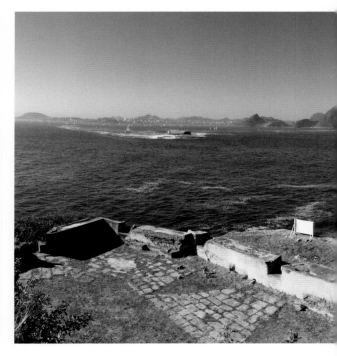

perb and unusual views of the city and the two private beaches that
e part of the site.

São José fort, originally built in 1565 and renovated in 1872, to-
ther with Santa Cruz fort, on the other side of Guanabara Bay at
iterói (which you can see clearly during the visit), was part of the
y's defence system. An interesting historical museum completes the
rt tour.

On the way back, you pass the remarkable Art Deco building that
as the first covered gymnasium in Latin America. Note the delightful
gures in Portuguese stone that celebrate different sports.

The tour ends at a remarkable site in every respect: the charming
aia de Fora, where Estácio de Sá berthed his ship on 1 March 1565
d founded the city. The foundation stone at the site, set back from the
ach, is a copy of the original, which is in the Igreja dos Capuchinhos
Capuchin church) at Tijuca.

Some people consider, therefore, that Ladeira São Sebastião, which
gins near the old Urca casino and ends at São José fort, is the oldest
reet in Rio.

Ipanema – Leblon – Lagoa – Gavea
Jardim botanico – Humaita

1. COFFEE ROUTE — 196
2. CAPELA DE NOSSA SENHORA DA CABEÇA — 198
3. STATUE OF THE *ORIXÁ* OSSANHA — 200
4. ENTRANCE TO THE ACADEMIA IMPERIAL DE BELAS ARTES — 202
5. GÁVEA ROUTE MARKERS — 204
6. ESOTERICISM OF THE BRAZILIAN FLAG — 206

⑦ OCCULT SIGNIFICANCE OF MORRO DOIS IRMÃOS 208

⑧ BUGLE BOY STATUE 210

⑨ VASE OF THE TRIUMPH OF GALATEA BY FRANÇOIS GIRARDON 212

⑩ PARQUE NATURAL MUNICIPAL DA CATACUMBA TO HUMAITÁ TRAIL 214

⑪ CENTRO NYINGMA DE BUDISMO TIBETANO 216

⑫ PARQUE DO MARTELO 218

COFFEE ROUTE

Historical route to the Christ statue

Trailhead: end of Rua Sarah Villela in Jardim Botânico
(21) 2491-1700 (Parque Nacional da Tijuca)
Distance and duration: 6km / 4h (well marked but difficult trail)
Free

The coffee route, different from Parque Lage's widely known path, the best way of reaching the Cristo Redentor (Christ the Redeemer). It winds through the lush vegetation of the Mata Atlântica (Atlantic forest), passing by two waterfalls, a colonial road and two watchtowers with breathtaking views. As a bonus, you're likely to come across marmosets (*Callithrix penicillata*) and other primates. But be aware that despite the excellent maintenance and signposting provided by the Tijuca Forest National Park in collaboration with volunteer groups Terra Limpa and Ecotribo, the trail is long and steep. It is advisable to set off early in the morning.

The trail starts at the end of Rua Sarah Villela. After the last house, it's another 200m or so to a small paved square, where the path begins. Although the first section is steep and signposted with yellow arrows, after about 10 minutes it joins the Transcarioca trail. At this junction, turn right. From there, just follow the yellow marks painted on rocks and trees.

After another 15-minute walk, the trail crosses the Primatas river opposite the first waterfall (Cachoeira dos Primatas). Just beyond the fork in the path, it's a good idea to climb up to the left and bathe in the second Primates' waterfall before retracing your steps to rejoin the Transcarioca trail. You'll pass the beautiful Lagoa viewpoint before arriving at Vale do Rio Cabeça.

This stretch is often frequented by groups of monkeys making a racket while swinging on branches and jumping from tree to tree. With a little luck you might also spot a toucan.

From Vale do Rio Cabeça the history of the trail grows richer. The fully paved route follows the contour lines. Note the remains of retaining walls, old houses and stone bridges. This road was built to transport coffee and other goods from Paneiras to Chácara do Rio Cabeça (so named because it was thought that the waters could cure migraine – *cabeça* meaning head).

According to the writings of Maria Graham in the early 19th century, Vale do Rio Cabeça hosted "extensive coffee plantations, interspersed with numerous orange, lemon and other shrubs that seem to be more a variation of the forest rather than a meeting of cultivated and wild land".

Thanks to the painstaking work of Thomás Nogueira da Gama, this region was completely reforested from 1862. A sharp eye will also be able to identify various exotic species such as jackfruit and some coffee plants.

Near Paneiras, the route passes close to a millennial fig tree, whose trunk is believed to be the largest of any on the Transcarioca trail.

Approaching the end of the path, you'll come to two forks, both well signposted. At the first one, keep right, while at the second you leave the main Transcarioca trail to turn left and follow the wooden arrows to 'Corcovado'. After crossing the railway track it's 10 more minutes to the Christ statue.

There are several options for the return trip: train, bus, walking down the route and the Transcarioca trail to Lage park, although this is not recommended for inexperienced hikers.

CAPELA DE NOSSA SENHORA DA CABEÇA

One of Rio's most delightful secrets

Rua Faro 80
Jardim Botânico
(21) 97237-2453
Monday to Saturday 10am–4pm
Mass 12 August, feast day of Our Lady of Cabeça, and other occasions

Not far from Rio's botanical gardens, hidden at the end of Rua Faro behind a large metal gate, the Casa Maternal Mello Mattos houses a school run by Carmelite nuns who also live there. Just ring the bell on weekdays, between 9am and 4pm, to share one of Rio's most delightful secrets: at the top of the hill stands a lovely little chapel built in 1603, one of the oldest buildings in Rio de Janeiro.

This serene chapel, whose atmosphere is conducive to prayer, will be opened for you on request.

It was built on the Engenho d'El Rey sugar plantation, which at the time extended over almost the entire area of what is now the Jardim Botânico. It was used as a private chapel by the estate owner, Governor Martim Correia, a member of whose family brought an image of Our Lady of Cabeça back from Portugal.

The story goes that St Euphrasius (1st century AD), the first bishop of the city of Andújar in southern Spain, received from the hands of St Peter a cedar statue of the Virgin, made by St Luke himself. On his return home, the bishop had a shrine built to house the statue. During the Muslim conquest of southern Spain, the local people hid this image in a cave on Monte Cabeça. It wasn't until 12 August 1227 that one Juan Alonso de Rivas, who had lost his right arm fighting the Muslims, discovered the hidden statue. The Virgin then restored his arm, a miracle that led to the rapid spread of the cult of Nossa Senhora da Cabeça (Our Lady of the Head), from the name of the hill where the statue had been found.

According to legend, the statue of Nossa Senhora da Cabeça was carved by St Luke, who lived at the time of the Virgin and probably knew her personally. It therefore possessed the immense distinction (like the crucifix of Lucca, in Tuscany, or the Holy Shroud of Turin, in the case of Jesus) of representing her *true* face. The original statue disappeared during the Spanish Civil War in 1937.

NEARBY
The fig tree in Rua Faro

At 51 Rua Faro, an imposing 300-year-old fig tree was threatened with being felled to make way for a new building. Defended by the residents' association (and its then president, Leonel Kaz), the fig tree has not only been preserved but is listed as heritage, thus becoming the first protected tree in the history of Brazil.

STATUE OF THE *ORIXÀ* OSSANHA ③

Rare image of an African-Brazilian deity in Rio

Jardim Botânico
Rua Jardim Botânico 1008
jbrj.gov.br
(21) 3874-1808
See timetables and admission charges on the Jardim Botânico website

At the far end of Rio's Botanical Garden, near the Rua Pacheco Leão exit in a rarely visited corner, is one of Rio's most intriguing statues, where followers of African-Brazilian traditions meet regularly.

The 5-metre-tall resin sculpture of Ossanha, an African-Brazilian deity or *orixá* (orisha), was designed in 2004 by artist Tatti Moreno, born on 18 December 1944 in Salvador de Bahia. A small sign at the statue's feet evokes the mystical and healing secrets of leaves and plants.

The *orixá* Ossanha (also known, according to various traditions, as Ossanyin, Ossaim, Ossãe or Ossain), as the deity of leaves and herbs, couldn't have found a better site in Rio than here in the Botanical Garden. He is symbolised by a metal rod terminating in seven points reaching for the sky. A bird soars from the central point.

The legend goes that Ossanha had received the secret of leaves from supreme god Olodumare. Ossanha knew that some leaves brought calmness or energy; others brought luck, glory, honours, or on the other hand misery, disease and accidents. Other *orixás* held no power over plants and depended on Ossanha to stay healthy and be successful in their endeavours.

Xangô (Shango), the impatient, impetuous warrior, annoyed by this state of affairs, plotted to steal the secret of plants from Ossanha. He explained to his wife Lansã that sometimes Ossanha hung a container on an iroko branch with his most powerful leaves inside. "Brew up a powerful storm on one of these days," Xangô told her. Lansã accepted the mission with alacrity.

The wind blew in great gusts, ripping the roofs from houses, uprooting trees, destroying everything in its path, and finally unhooking the container from where it was hanging. It was carried far away and the leaves all flew out.

The *orixás* recovered them all. Each *orixá* became the owner of certain leaves, but Ossanha remained the "master of the secret" of their virtues and the words that had to be said to activate them.

ENTRANCE TO THE ACADEMIA IMPERIAL DE BELAS ARTES

A movable feast for the eyes

Jardim Botânico – Rua Jardim Botânico 1008
jbrj.gov.br – (21) 3874-1808
See timetables and admission charges on the Jardim Botânico website
Bus: 105, 109, 112, 309, 410, 439, 538, 548, 584 and 585

I n Rio's Botanical Garden, at the end of Barbosa Rodrigues avenue lined with its immense imperial palms and bamboo, stands the impos ing neoclassical entrance to the former Imperial Academy of Fine Art This entrance was not always here; designed in the early 19th centur

French architect Auguste-Henri-Victor Grandjean de Montigny, it
is moved to the gardens in 1938 when the city centre Academy was
molished to make way for the Ministry of Finance, which was even-
ally built elsewhere (see p. 64). Today, the former site of the Academy
a car park.

After the Portuguese court moved to Rio in 1808, major scientif-
expeditions visited the country. In March 1816 the Missão Artística
ancesa (French Artistic Mission) sailed to Rio to teach art and archi-
cture. The 40 members of the mission, including Jean-Baptiste Debret
d Grandjean de Montigny, had a strong academic background. The
cademy was founded the same year but was not inaugurated until 1826
der the name Academia Imperial de Belas Artes. In the 20th century
e Academy was absorbed by the Federal University of Rio de Janeiro
d became known as the Escola de Belas Artes (School of Fine Arts).

Mestre Valentim at the Botanical Garden

In the violet nursery in the centre of the park, a memorial to Mestre
Valentim preserves the remains of two of his wonderful fountains.
These are the statues of Echo and Narcissus, the first cast metal
sculptures in Brazil.

They originally formed part of the Marrecas fountain, installed
in 1785 at the junction of Rua das Belas Noites (later Rua das
Marrecas because of the fountain) and what is now Rua Evaristo da
Veigam towards the main entrance to the Passeio Público (Public
Promenade, see p. 112).

The other two works on display are sculptures of wading birds
(egrets or herons), which formerly graced the *Fonte dos Jacarés*
(Caiman fountain) on the Passeio Público, opened in 1783.

Near the Academy entrance and the *pernambuco* (brazil-wood)
grove, you can see the gateway of the Real Fábrica de Pólvora
(Royal Gunpowder Factory) and the Oficina do Moinho dos Pilões
(Workshop of the Pressing Mill).

The factory was founded in 1808 by Dom João and occupied the
former headquarters of Engenho Rodrigo de Freitas sugar cane
presses. The gateway and some sections of wall are all that remain.
At the entrance to the workshop, known as the Casa dos Pilões
(House of the Presses) where the powder was compressed, you can
still see the great stone wheels that were used to grind coal and
sulphur.

There is a small museum and archaeological site there now.

GÁVEA ROUTE MARKERS

Forgotten route markers

Opposite Estrada da Gávea 10
Bus: 170, 537, 538, 539

Opposite number 10 Estrada de Gávea stands one of the rou markers erected in the city in the 1930s. You can still pick o the directions on both sides, "R.M.S. Vicente 01" (Rua Marques de S Vicente) and "Av. Niemeyer" (this one obscured by graffiti). The initi "PDF" (Prefecture of the Federal District), dating from the time wh Rio was the capital of the Republic, are inscribed on the other side.

These markers were used to measure distances between location "from 1,000 in 1,000 metres", as specified by the road signage regu tions of 1928.

Over time, they have lost some of the reasons for their existence and any have been withdrawn. Today, research shows that thirty-four of ese "forgotten" markers are still at their original sites.

Most of them are in the western suburbs of Rio (mainly at Cam-• Grande, Guaratiba and Sepetiba), but some can also be seen in the •rth and on the roads Vista Chinesa, Joá and ineiras in the middle of juca forest. The mark- on Estrada da Gávea ems to be the only one 't in the city's southern ne.

The Circuit de Gávea, a motor race known around the world and held between 1933 and 1954 (with a break during the Second World War), skirted Morro Dois Irmãos. The circuit of approximately 11 km began at Rua Marques de São Vicente (the start was near what is now the Gávea shopping centre). It continued along Bartolomeu Mitre, Visconde de Albuquerque and Niemeyer avenues, as far as Estrada da Gávea, via what is now Rocinha and down to the route marker. With over a hundred bends and a variety of road surfaces (asphalt, cement, paving stones, sand), the circuit has seen many serious accidents.

A motor race that inspired a March of the Rio carnaval

In 1937, Germany was represented by legendary driver Hans Stuck racing under the Nazi flag.

The race was eventually won by the Italian Carlo Pintacuda, who became the "Hero of Gávea" of his day. In Carioca slang, Pintacuda means "courage" or "bold".

Years later, during the 1950 Carnaval, it inspired the "March of the Stutterer" ("I'm s-soft when I s-speak / But I'm a Pintucada when I kiss").

Since independence, Brazil has mainly been represented by two flags: the old flag of the Empire and the new flag of the Republic.

In 1822, the Brazilian imperial flag had a green background with a central yellow diamond, within which a green coat of arms consisted of a circle containing 19 stars (representing the states). At the centre of this circle, an armillary sphere was set on the Cross of the Order of Christ.

Above the coat of arms was the crown of the Empire of Brazil. Below, two interlaced branches (coffee and tobacco plants) climbed up the sides. The green and yellow colours were chosen by Emperor Dom Pedro I in person: green for his family, the royal house of Bragança; and yellow for the Habsburg family of his first wife, Maria Leopoldina of Austria.

Pedro I commissioned the design from renowned French artist Jean-Baptiste Debret (1768–1848), a Freemason who had associated himself in the meantime with Brazilian Masonry through the minister José Bonifácio de Andrada e Silva. The artist would have greatly influenced the emperor in his choice of colours, which were, indeed, those of the secret society he'd founded, the *Nobre Ordem dos Cavaleiros da Santa Cruz* (Noble Order of the Knights of the Holy Cross), known as the *Apostalado* (Apostolate), to which the ruler belonged under the title of Archon, Head of the Apostolate. It was opposed both to absolute monarchy and to a secular republic and envisaged an ideal state where the emperor would be a sage (symbolised by the colour yellow) in a kingdom of peace and creativity (symbolised by the colour green). The Apostolate was closed down on 23 June 1823.

Later, on 19 November 1889, following a proposal from Benjamin Constant, a provisional government decree approved the current national flag of Brazil, keeping the structure of the imperial flag, bearing the inscription *Ordem e Progresso* (Order and Progress) inspired by the maxim of Positivist philosopher Auguste Comte: "Love as a principle and order as the basis; progress as the goal". The yellow and green flag was designed by painter Décio Vilares. It consists of a green rectangle symbolising the Brazilian forests and in the centre a yellow diamond evoking the country's mineral wealth, especially gold. The blue starry sphere in the centre of the diamond represents the astronomical aspect of the Rio de Janeiro sky at 8.30am on 15 November 1889, the day of the Proclamation of the Republic. This sphere originally contained 21 stars (currently 27), symbolising the national states and the federal district.

These stars on the flag are not just for decorative effect, but have a real esoteric meaning. According to the Egyptian Hermetic tradition, rediscovered in Europe in the Renaissance (see *Secret Florence* in this series of guides), which was well known to Brazilian Freemasons and Positivists: "That which is below is like that which is above and that which is above is like that which is below." This correspondence between the macrocosm and the microcosm means that the representation of the sky at a given date on the ceiling of a room (as in some palaces and churches in Rome, and Florence in particular) or a flag, as here, is expected to attract celestial energy in the place of representation. Representing it on a flag to be flown throughout the country was meant, in the minds of its creators, to attract celestial energies to the entire Brazilian territory.

Critics, however, say that the arrangement of stars is the reverse of the constellations visible in the Southern Hemisphere. The flag is, in fact, a mirror that reflects the night sky, hence the reversal of positions and astral correlation.

Don't forget that Emperor Dom Pedro II, as well as astronomers Luís Cruls and Manuel Pereira Reis, and of course Décio Vilares himself, were keen astrologers and they placed the stars on the flag with the constitutional support of the Brazilian Masonic Order in which the Republican Club of Master Mason Lopes Trovão played a leading role.

PARÁ
Spica (α Virginis)
AMAZONAS
Prócion (α Canis Minoris)
MATO GROSSO DO SUL
Alphard (α Hydrae)
RONDÔNIA
Wezen (δ Canis Majoris)
MATO GROSSO
Sírio (α Canis Majoris)
RORAIMA
Muliphen (γ Canis Majoris)
AMAPÁ
Mirzam (β Canis Majoris)
TOCANTIS
Adhara (ε Canis Majoris)
GOIÁS
Canopus (γ Carinae)
BAHIA
Gacrux (γ Crucis)
MINAS GERAIS
Pálida (δ Crucis)
ESPÍRITO SANTO
Intrometida (ε Crucis)
SÃO PAULO
Acrux (α Crucis)

14. ACRE
Dhanab al Shuja (γ Hydrae)
15. PIAUÍ
Antares (α Scorpii)
16. MARANHÃO
Graffias (β Scorpii)
17. CEARÁ
Wei (ε Scorpii)
18. RIO GRANDE DO NORTE
Shaula (λ Scorpii)
19. PARAÍBA
Girtab (κ Scorpii)
20. PERNAMBUCO
Denebakrab (μ Scorpii)
21. ALAGOAS
Sargas (θ Scorpii)
22. SERGIPE
Apollyon (ι Scorpii)
23. SANTA CATARINA
δ Trianguli Australis
24. RIO GRANDE DO SUL
Atria (α Trianguli Australis)
25. PARANÁ
γ Trianguli Australis
26. RIO DE JANEIRO
Mimosa (β Crucis)
27. BRASÍLIA
Polaris Australis (σ Octantis)

Occult significance of Morro Dois Irmãos

Long before Ipanema acquired its present characteristics, *Morro Dois Irmãos* (Two Brothers hill) had already caught the attention of the Tupinambás, members of the Tupí tribe who lived on the coast. They devoted a special cult to the rock, described in Capuchin chronicles along with the local legends associated with it. Even the name Ipanema, "unclean water" (not fit to drink, referring to the salt water of the nearby ocean), is Tupí in origin.

Tupí religious culture was based on nature worship, in which stone shapes were very important. Such was the case of this peak, whose cone is superimposed on another triangular shape. The pair were associated very early on with Jacy (Moon, Woman) and Tupan (Sun, Man), in other words the Earth's two main stars that punctuate day and night, the activity of the body and the repose of the soul. They were nicknamed the *irmãos* (siblings).

The celebration of this stone cult was practised by the indigenous people in the following way: in the highlands, they worshipped the Sun (Tupan) with dances and war chants evoking the solar force where men dominated; and in the lowlands, they worshipped the Moon (Jacy) with dances and songs evoking maternal energy, represented by the waters of the ocean and led by women. As they needed a totemic symbol of the two celestial bodies, the rocky mound or Upabanem (Ipanema) with its suggestive contours was chosen.

But the story doesn't stop there: in the 16th century, the present region of Rio de Janeiro and Niteroi was occupied by the Tupinambá tribe of the Termiminós, whose chief was the famous Arariboia. Born around 1523, he helped the Portuguese to expel the French and their Tamoios allies from the region by his decisive victory at the battle of Uruçu-mirim (now Flamengo beach) on 20 January 1567. In return for his support, Arariboia received from the King of Portugal, Dom Sebastião, the cross and coat of a Knight of the Order of Christ. He was also given a woman of mixed Portuguese and Brazilian blood, with whom he had a large number of offspring who later interbred with the family of Antonio de Mariz Coutinho (Barcelos, 1537–Brazil 1584). Arariboia converted to Christianity and took the name Martim Afonso de Souza, in homage to the Portuguese navigator. He died in 1574. In order to perpetuate the memory of heroic Arariboia and his wife, who had contributed so much to the Brazilian people, shortly after his death the Termiminós decided that Morro Dois Irmãos represented their great leader and his wife, incarnations of Tupan and Jacy, the supreme deities of the Tupí pantheon.

Some even go further back in time to claim that the name "Morro

Dois Irmãos", which dominates Pedra da Gávea, evokes the memory of "Phoenician Brazil". In 1000 BC Baal-Zir, the exiled King of Tyre, capital of Phoenicia, is thought to have arrived here with his court and family, including his twin children, the boy Yet-Baal-Bey and the girl Yet-Baal-Bel. The memory of these two would be perpetuated in the name "Morro Dois Irmãos", which along with Pedra da Gávea formed a triad of stones symbolising the Sun, Moon and Earth. Legend or not, the fact is that the Phoenicians were the greatest navigators of early history and reached the most distant lands of the Western Sea (the Atlantic) according to several historians. And in their religion, these three celestial bodies played a decisive role, especially the Sun called Baal (Lord), the same meaning that the Tupí gave to Tupan.

A magical memory of Rio de Janeiro's forgotten past, Morro Dois Irmãos is still there, shrouded by mysterious mists, effacing time. Even São Paulo singer Chico Buarque admits: *Dois Irmãos, quando vai alta a madrugada / E a teus pés vão-se encostar os instrumentos / Aprenti a respeitar tua prumada / E desconfiar do teu silêncio* (Two Brothers off to the heights at dawn / And your feet facing the instruments / I learned to respect your peaks / And be wary of your silence).

BUGLE BOY STATUE

Memories of Bahia in Ipanema

Corner of Rua Visconde de Pirajá and Rua Garcia D'Ávila
Metro: Nossa Senhora da Paz

At the corner of Visconde de Pirajá and Garcia D'Ávila streets, ne
the electricity pole, is a curious bronze statue of a soldier blowing
bugle, his foot resting on a cannon half-buried in the sidewalk.

This caricature is in tribute to Corporal Luís Lopes, bugler to th
Brazilian forces fighting for independence in the province of Bah
1822–1823.

Unveiled in 2004, the unusual style of the statue caused some contr
versy. Even the story of Corporal Luis and his role in the battle of Pirajá
8 November 1822 is controversial.

The battle wasn't going well for the Brazilians, who were outnumbere
by the Portuguese. Their commander Major José de Barros Falcão, sensin
imminent defeat, ordered the bugler to sound the retreat.

The corporal disobeyed orders and instead sounded the 'cavalry, a
vance and behead'. Luís Lopes surprised and panicked the Portugues

who dispersed, giving the adva
tage to the Brazilian troops.

In the absence of official do
uments, some claim that this i
cident never happened. But th
poem *Paraguaçu* by Ladislau Tit
ro, an eyewitness to the battle
Pirajá, mentions the feat of Lu
Lopes.

There is no doubt that th
Brazilians won this battle, fina
defeating the Portuguese on 2 J
ly 1823, ten months after Do
Pedro I had declared indepen
ence on the banks of the Ipiran
river in São Paulo on 7 Septemb
1822.

Another Ipanema tribute to Bahia's independence heroes

When the neighbourhood was urbanised after the founding of Vila Ipanema in 1884, many streets paid tribute to family members and friends of the entrepreneurs José Antonio Moreira Filho, Baron of Ipanema, and Antonio José da Silva. In 1922, during the independence centenary celebrations, the names of some streets were changed to honour the heroes who had fought in the War of Independence. Rua Otávio Silva, for example, became Rua Maria Quitéria and Rua 20 Novembro, which commemorated the birthday of the baron's wife, was changed to Rua Visconde de Pirajá.

Maria Quitéria (1792–1853) is the 'woman soldier of Brazil'. When she learned of the struggle for independence, she ran away from home, cut off her long hair, disguised herself as a man and enlisted as a volunteer in the armed forces of Bahia.

Joana Angélica (1761–1822), martyr, succumbed to the blows of Portuguese soldiers' bayonets in attempting to defend the convent of Lapa, in Salvador, where she was mother superior.

Visconde de Pirajá: perhaps the most important leader of the movement was Joaquim Pires de Carvalho e Albuquerque (1788–1848), a wealthy landowner known as 'Colonel Santinho'. He received the title of Viscount (Visconde) of Pirajá after his victory on home soil.

Barão de Jaguaripe: Francisco Elesbão Pires de Carvalho e Albuquerque (1787–1856) consolidated the independence of Bahia and was proclaimed president of the revolutionary junta that governed the province. He was the Viscount of Pirajá's brother.

Barão da Torre: Antonio Joaquim Pires de Carvalho e Albuquerque (1774–1852), whose full title was Barão da Torre (Baron of the Tower) of Garcia D'Ávila, turned his castle into an operational base for the independence forces. Another brother of the Visconde de Pirajá, he also became his son in-law when he married one of the viscount's daughters.

VASE OF THE TRIUMPH OF GALATEA BY FRANÇOIS GIRARDON

An exceptional copy of a vase in the Louvre

Praça José de Acioli
Metro: Nossa Senhora da Paz

Despite what some might think, Rio is not just breathtaking landscapes, although some of its artworks are almost overwhelmed by the beauty of their surroundings. If proof were needed, on the shores of Lagoa Rodrigo de Freitas in Ipanema is a round plaza with stunning views of the lagoon, Corcovado in the background and Cristo Redentor in the heights. An unusual marble vase with a strange history has stood in this little plaza for over 60 years, covered with a thick layer of plaster.

Recently the prefecture decided to give the vase a facelift and discovered that the plaster actually concealed a very fine piece of artistically carved Carrara marble, on which they had no information. When was it made and by whom? How did it arrive here? And why was it plastered over?

An Ipanema resident eventually came across the original vase at the Louvre in Paris. The *Triomphe de Galatée* (Triumph of Galatea) was one of a pair commissioned by Louis XIV in 1683 for the gardens of Versailles. After 200 years in the royal gardens the vase was transferred to Saint-Cloud near Paris, where it stood for several years until the Louvre gave it a home in 1872. It can still be seen there today.

A few copies of this vase have turned up in major art collections around the world, including the Wallace Collection in London. Some have been offered for sale in international auctions. They are usually made from cheaper materials, such as earthenware or bronze. The only known marble copy is this one in Ipanema. It is of exceptional quality and most likely dates from the 19th century.

PARQUE NATURAL MUNICIPAL DA CATACUMBA TO HUMAITÁ TRAIL

10

Effort in / beauty out

Lagoa
(21) 2247-9949 – Admission free

The stretch of the Transcarioca trail from Catacumba park to Humaitá shows the clearest link between "effort in" and "beauty out" of all Rio's landscapes. Taking advantage of the steps and the ruins of the Catacumba *favela* – razed in 1970 to make way for a sculpture park (decorated with striking work by, among others, Carybé, Frans Krajcberg and Bruno Giorgi) – the trail was opened in 1997.

The layout, which is well marked and maintained, runs by the sculptures before entering the forest, the result of successful reforestation and proof that it's possible to recuperate run-down areas. The ascent is by the steep stone paths of the former favela, with some stopping points where information boards tell the story of the *favela*, reforestation and wildlife such as silvery marmosets and toucans.

After half an hour's walk you arrive at Sacopã belvedere, which rises 134 m and offers one of the best views of Rio, taking in Pedra da Gávea, Morro Dois Irmãos, Ipanema beach, Christ the Redeemer, the Botanical Garden and Rodrigo de Freitas lagoon.

From here the trail continues to Urubu belvedere, where in addition to the spectacular view, you can also abseil (Lagoa Aventuras (21) 4105-0079 / 7870-9162).

Next, the path descends a flight of steps from the former *favela* before branching out in two directions: to the right, you'll reach Catacumba park by the same path; to the left, the hike (much less known) continues for an hour on the Transcarioca path towards the community of Cabritos, on the highest point of Rua Vitória Régia at Humaitá. This second section has recently been taken over by the maintenance team from Catacumba park. It runs along the rock via wooden stairways and *vias ferratas* ("iron ways").

Although a guide isn't essential you need some experience and to be in good physical condition.

Along this route, you can see more views of Rodrigo de Freitas lagoon and tropical plants such as bromeliads and cacti clinging to the bare rock.

CENTRO NYINGMA
DE BUDISMO TIBETANO

A voyage back in time

Rua Casuarina 297
(21) 2527-9388 – instituto@nyingmario.org.br
Meditation on Sunday morning 9am–10am, Monday at 8pm, Tuesday at 7pm
Thursday at 8.45pm
Recitation of mantras Sunday 10am–11am
Other occasional open days – check with the centre's website: nyingmario.org.b

Hidden in the foothills of Morro da Saudade, the Nyingma Tibetan Buddhism Centre is one of the best kept secrets of Lagoa. From Rua Fonte da Saudade, follow Rua Bogari until you reach Rua Casuaria. Just past the barrier, a wooden door on the left guards the entrance to the temple.

The entrance is the most spectacular part of the centre; deep within the small courtyard, a stupa (Buddhist traditional monument housing sacred relics) welcomes visitors against a background of the Corcovado statue of Christ – a lovely symbol of communion between religions.

The lie of the land gives you a real feeling of immersion in almost virgin nature, despite the tops of two buildings glimpsed down below. Framed by the centre and its prayer flags, the spectacle of stupa, forest, rock and Christ is an invitation to meditate for a moment on the benches provided.

The centre welcomes visitors several times a week for meditation sessions or mantra recitations. During our visit, the mantras left us with a deep sense of well-being.

Where does the name Fonte da Saudade *come from?*

The *Fonte da Saudade* (Fountain of Sorrow) neighbourhood takes its name from a fountain that really did exist. Until the early 19th century, women came to do their laundry there, a few steps from what used to be Piaçava beach. It was also from here, before Rua Jardim Botânico had been constructed, that Prince Regent Dom João took the boat to the Botanical Garden on his way from Botafogo.

The water of the fountain had legendary magical properties; anyone drinking it could never forget the beauty of the place. The fountain was demolished when land was reclaimed from the lagoon during works carried out under Mayor Carlos Sampaio (1920–1922). A reproduction has since been installed at number 111 Rua Fonte da Saudade.

PARQUE DO MARTELO

Hidden treasure of Humaitá

Rua Miguel Pereira 41
(21) 2527-0177
Daily 8.30am–1pm
No pets allowed
Admission free

Strolling along the charming Rua Miguel Pereira with its many houses and small buildings, you could easily pass the wooden gate number 41 without realising this is the entrance to a little-known urban treasure trove: Martelo park, with its gardens, fruit trees, shrubs, children's playground and physical exercise space.

The 16,000m² park on the slopes of Morro do Martelo, situated within a residential area, is the result of the local people's long struggle to block a 200-apartment development. In the successful conclusion to this 'war' the prefecture ceded the site to the residents' association of upper Hamaitá, provided they took over the maintenance of the site. The park opened in May 2005.

Once you're through the gate and access ramp, the atmosphere is one of near perfect tranquility, rare in Rio. There's a feeling of intimacy, as if you were in the garden of your own house. Indeed, there is a natural division between the children's playground and sports facilities and the rampant foliage climbing up the hill. Those who venture to the top can enjoy a panorama of the Lagoa neighbourhood and the ocean beyond Ipanema. The park, used mainly by locals, also offers a splendid view of Cristo Redentor (Christ the Redeemer) just above.

Next to the playground and outdoor shower is the administrative building where events are organised. The upkeep of the park depends on contributions from local residents and fundraising activities.

Before this zone was turned into a park, for half of the 20th century it was a small favela. Later it was the site of a workshop and engineering company.

As well as local residents, the battle for the park was supported by personalities such as landscaper Burle Marx, architect Oscar Niemeyer and poets Ferreira Gullar and Carlos Drummond de Andrade, who were among the signatories of a document on 15 September 1984 declaring that *"the residents' cause ... means for the city, for the community and for the neighbourhood, the preservation of a zone that constitutes ... a landscape and cultural heritage"*.

Joatinga – São Contrado – Barra da Tijuca – West

1. HANGAR DO ZEPPELIN — 222
2. "SENTA A PUA" MEMORIAL — 226
3. PONTE DOS JESUÍTAS — 228
4. WALLACE FOUNTAIN — 229
5. 1ST BATALHÃO DE ENGENHARIA DE COMBATE — 230
6. RUINS OF THE IMPERIAL SLAUGHTERHOUSE — 232
7. PALACETE PRINCESA ISABEL — 233
8. MARKER NUMBER 7 OF THE ESTRADA REAL (ROYAL ROAD) — 234
9. CAPELA MAGDALENA — 236

10. TRANSCARIOCA TRAIL TO THE WILD BEACHES
    OF GRUMARI   238
11. STATUE OF A FOOTBALL PLAYER   240
12. BUMBA-MEU-BOI HOUSE/MUSEUM   242
13. MUSEU BISPO DO ROSÁRIO   244
14. AÇUDE TRAIL   246
15. TRANSCARIOCA TRAIL, FROM ALTO DA BOA VISTA
    TO MESA DO IMPERADOR   248
16. THE MYSTERIOUS INSCRIPTION ON PEDRA DA GÁVEA   251

HANGAR DO ZEPPELIN

The world's only operational airship hangar

Santa Cruz Air Force Base
Rua do Imperio
(21) 3078-0305
Wednesday 9am–11.30am by reservation only, by e-mail (scs.basc@fab.1000.br),
state name and number of people
Train Santa Cruz; Bus (BRT) Santa Cruz
From either station (they are close together), take bus 849 (from the air base gate
to the monument, about 800 metres)

The Zeppelin Hangar, the only one in the world today built for large-dimension airships, is indisputably the historical footnote to Santa Cruz Air Force Base.

Visitors to the base will find the hangar 800 m from the gate, together with a small aluminium reproduction of the zeppelin. Despite the military housing and other buildings, the tour provokes strong emotions. This vast space, set against the distant Serra do Mar mountain range, is battered by relentless winds and subjected to the rhythm of fighter jets landing and taking off, as the runway is next to the imposing hangar.

The Art Deco building, 270 m long, 50 m wide and 60 m high,

is listed as a national heritage site. Originally known as Bartolomeu de Gusmão Airport – in tribute to the Portuguese priest (born in Brazil) who researched ballooning in the early 18th century – it was built to accommodate the huge German airships *Graf Zeppelin* and *Hindenburg* that serviced the Frankfurt–Rio route. Opened on 26 December 1936, the hangar stopped receiving zeppelins as a consequence of the *Hindenburg* fire in May 1937 at New Jersey.

80-tonne doors

The electrical connections in the hangar have a special coating to prevent sparks that could ignite an airship.

The roof is still the original, despite being exposed to very challenging climatic conditions. The smallest door, used for ventilation, was intended for moving the landing stage around.

The airships entered and exited through the main doorway, whose doors weigh 80 tonnes each and take six minutes to open to 60 degrees.

The control tower, on the top of the hangar, offers a view from the port of Sepetiba to the Guandu river.

The gigantic hangar was only used for nine trips: four by the *LZ 129 Hindenburg* and five by the *LZ 127 Zeppelin*.

A hydrogen plant had also been built to power the airships, as well as a railway line connecting the hangar to Central do Brasil station. After the end of airship operations and the outbreak of the Second World War in 1939, the Brazilian government took over the site, which in 1941 became the Santa Cruz Air Force Base. Part of the hangar is still used for fighter aircraft maintenance.

Two airships and a bicycle

A visit to the hangar begins with the "historical room", small but very informative, offering photos and details of the airships: each had 45 crew members and could comfortably carry 35 (*Graf Zeppelin*) or 50 (*Hindenburg*) passengers. There were 200 workers, nicknamed "spiders", dispersed over the runway to help move the airships around.

Also on display is an unusual bicycle, a tribute to Seu Mouzinho, who helped to build the hangar. With his experience in the general workings of the base, he was employed there until his death in 1998 and went everywhere on this bicycle. His house is now a small museum displaying the personal effects of someone who had an intimate knowledge of the history of the hangar, airships and the military base.

© Rcandre

"SENTA A PUA" MEMORIAL

A little-known monument by Oscar Niemeyer

Santa Cruz Air Force Base
Rua do Imperio
(21) 3078-0305
Wednesday 9am–11.30am by reservation only, by e-mail (scs.basc@fab.1000.br):
state name and number of people
Train Santa Cruz; Bus (BRT) Santa Cruz
From either station (they are close together), take bus 849 (from the air base gate
to the monument, about 800 metres)

On the Air Force base – the home of Brazilian fighter planes and site of the spectacular Zeppelin Hangar (see p. 222) – a little-known memorial pays tribute to Brazilian airmen who fought in the Second World War. This is a forgotten project designed by architect Oscar Niemeyer.

Niemeyer's reinforced concrete conception, painted white to emphasise the spaces and increase the contrast between light and shadow, recalls the trajectory and impact of the bombs dropped by P-47 Thunrbolt aircraft of the 1st Fighter Group of the "Senta a Pua" squadron.

The inner part of the memorial lists the names of all the pilots in the uadron and houses the mausoleum of its first commander, Brigadier ero Moura.

On the outside, the symbol "Senta a Pua" stands out, with an explanation of its meaning.

Alongside the memorial, you'll discover something rarely seen on finished work: Niemeyer's drawings and original texts explaining his oncept. The P-47 flown by Lieutenant Lima Mendes, who completed nety-four missions during the war, forms part of the monument.

"Senta a Pua" is the witty logo created by Flight Captain Fortunato âmara de Oliveira, when the group was still training in the United ates before leaving for Italy.

The choice of an emblem sparked many discussions among the pits. Fortunato suggested *Avestruz Voadora* (Flying Ostrich), a choice ey all agreed with.

The ostrich certainly isn't a flying creature, but its speed and agility presented the Brazilian pilot in action. Moreover, it can stomach any pe of food, including American! That at least is what the pilots jokingsaid; they did indeed find the GI rations very strange, although they t used to them.

The ostrich is a caricature of one of these men, Lieutenant Lima Iendes. The motto comes from "Senta a Pua, Zé Maria" (literally,

ou'll feel my club it you hard], Zé Ma-a"), a very popular ying in the 1940s, pecially in Northeast razil.

It was also used by lots who, on their way the air base, shouted the driver: "Senta a ua, Zé Maria!"

The memorial was unveiled on 22 April 2001, Fighter Planes Day. This commemoration has been held on that date since 1945, when in the skies over Italy the 1st Fighter Group clocked up the greatest number of missions in a single day.

PONTE DOS JESUÍTAS

The third monument to be listed as part of the country's historic heritage

Estrada do Curtume, Santa Cruz
Train: Santa Cruz; Bus (BRT): Santa Cruz
From either of the adjacent stations, take bus 807

On a bend on the road to Curtume, comfortably installed among lush pastures, a stone bridge is an unexpected sight as there is no longer a river. Originally known as the Guandu river bridge, and then the Pedro I bridge, the Bridge of the Jesuits is one of the finest examples of 18th century Rio de Janeiro architecture. It was built in 1752 on the land of Fazenda de Santa Cruz, the Jesuit agricultural estate, as a means of crossing the Guandu river and regulating its flow by diverting the water to the Itaguaí river when necessary.

As well as protecting crops and herds, this bridge/dam mitigated the risk of flood damage to housing. Changing the course of the Guandu river – today, the main source of the city's water supply – means that the bridge has lost its purpose but it remains an important architectural monument.

During its construction, two Jesuits went to Holland to study methods of controlling water flow. The 50-metre-long and 6-metre-wide bridge was built from stone, with lime from oyster shells and fine sand. The columns, with their integrated guardrails, have Portuguese cone-shaped capitals. The base of the bridge, also stone, has four arches that allowed the volume of water to be controlled.

In the centre of the bridge stands the seal of the Society of Jesus with the Latin insignia IHS (Jesus Saviour of Men). Another Latin inscription above, engraved in the stone, warns visitors: "Kneel down before such a great name, traveller. Here also is bowed the river in spate."

In its time, the Bridge of the Jesuits (restored in 2008) was a benchmark of hydraulic engineering on a massive scale. It is the third monument to be listed as part of the nation's historic heritage.

© Halley Pacheco de Oliveira

WALLACE FOUNTAIN ④

A Parisian fountain in Santa Cruz

Praça Dom Romualdo, Santa Cruz
Train: Santa Cruz
Bus (BRT): Santa Cruz
From either of the adjacent stations, take bus 872A

During the second half of the 19th century, the English philanthropist Richard Wallace (1818–1890) offered Paris and other cities a hundred water fountains, which came to be known as "Wallace fountains". Rio de Janeiro received three of them.

The fountain in Praça Dom Romualdo at Santa Cruz originally stood in front of the former Paço Imperial of Santa Cruz (see p. 230), today Battalion Villagran Cabrita. The other two are currently in Parque da Cidade at Gávea and in the Manacás garden, Tijuca forest.

© Rcandre

Built by the famous artistic metalworks at Val d'Osne, France, these castiron fountains were designed by Charles Lebourg (1829–1906). They are decorated with statues of four draped female figures, symboling the virtues of kindness, charity, sobriety and simplicity. On the base of each fountain is the signature of its creator: Ch. Lebourg SC 1872 – Val d'Osne.

Although the water supply doesn't seem to work any longer, the fountain in Praça Dom Romualdo has been in good condition since it was renovated in 2012.

Given the shape and vast size of the Igreja Matriz (mother church) de Nossa Senhora da Conceição near the fountain, some residents jokingly claim that its architecture reminds them of the Zeppelin Hangar (see p. 222), also in Santa Cruz. It is, in fact, inspired by the beautiful Igreja de São Francisco de Assis (Church of Saint Francis of Assisi, known as Igreja da Pampulha, Belo Horizonte, 1943), an iconic project by modernist architect Oscar Niemeyer, without having the same aesthetic qualities.

1ST BATALHÃO DE ENGENHARIA DE COMBATE

A monastery that became an imperial palace then a military academy

Praça Ruão 35 – (21) 3513-5100
Monday to Thursday 9am–11am and 1pm–4pm: go to the head office and ask
for the Public Relations department
Train Santa Cruz; Bus (BRT) Santa Cruz
On arriving at either station (they are close together), take the right-hand side
of the passage over the railway line and continue on foot to Praça Ruão

The former Paço Imperial (Imperial Palace) in Praça Ruão, San Cruz, has an impeccably preserved facade, even if the interior bea little trace of its origins.

Today the headquarters of the 1st Battalion School of Military E gineering, known as Battalion Villagran Cabrita, the building's obscu history began in the 16th century when the land fell into the hands the Jesuits. They founded the agricultural estate of Fazenda de San Cruz and by 1751 (the date is still visible on the main gate) a chap and monastery had been constructed. In 1759, with the expulsion the Jesuits from Portuguese territories, the property was returned to th Portuguese Crown. After the arrival of the royal family in Rio in 180 the monastery was renovated to become in 1811 the Paço Real (Roy Palace) of Santa Cruz. It was designed for the greater comfort of Do João, who remained there for months, holding public audiences an even organising receptions.

After Brazil declared independence from Portugal in 1822, the site
became known as the Paço Imperial (Imperial Palace). Another floor
was then added to the building. Dom Pedro II, owner of two telephones
presented to him by Alexander Graham Bell, installed South America's
first phone line, which connected the royal palaces of São Cristóvão
and Santa Cruz. Brazil's first post office was also built in Santa Cruz in
1843 on the Rua do Comércio, now Rua Senador Camará. The imperial
slaughterhouse (see p. 232), meanwhile, was opened in 1881.

During the 19th century, renowned artists such as the Frenchman
Jean-Baptiste Debret, the Austrian Thomas Ender and the Englishwom-
an Maria Graham were welcome visitors to the palace. Reproductions
of their paintings still hang in the "Green Room". There is also a small
picture showing changes to the building, including the addition of the
third floor, carried out during the Republican period when the property
was nationalised.

After Brazil's proclamation of independence on the banks of the
Ipiranga river in São Paulo, Dom Pedro I commemorated the occasion at Santa Cruz palace with members of his court, before re-
turning to São Cristóvão.

The cross that gave its name to a neighbourhood

On the lawn in front of the palace stands a wooden cross, a reproduction of the one installed by the Jesuits that gave its name to the
neighbourhood.
There is also a stone route marker, one of twelve along the Estrada
Real (Royal Road) of Santa Cruz (Holy Cross) that connected the
region to the city (see p. 234).

Agricultural estate of Santa Cruz

The Fazenda de Santa Cruz, a Jesuit property dating from 1589,
used thousands of slaves.
In its heyday, there were twenty-two enclosures for various types of
livestock and a wide range of plantations. The property had over 25
workshops with the most up-to-date facilities to meet every need,
as well as a hospital, schools and even an orchestra and choir, in
which the slaves played and sang. The country's first conservatoire
of music was founded here.

RUINS OF THE IMPERIAL SLAUGHTERHOUSE

The slaughterhouse that was once the most modern in the world

Fundação de Apoio à Escola Técnica (FAETEC – Foundation for Technical School Support) – Largo do Bodegão 46, Santa Cruz
Monday to Friday 8am–4pm – Visits on reservation: (21) 2333-7228 (Free)
Train: Santa Cruz; Bus (BRT): Santa Cruz, then 20-minute walk or any bus line to Sepetiba

A t its inauguration by Dom Pedro II in 1881, the Santa Cruz slaugh terhouse in Praça Bodegão was considered to be the most moderi in the world. The Palacete do Matadouro (slaughterhouse palace) and tl Vila Operária (workers' village) were built alongside each other. Whi the palace is today a vibrant cultural centre, only the ruins of the slaugl terhouse remain and the workers' housing has lost all its character. Ti ruins of the "slaughter route" and slaughterhouse are overgrown by tre and undergrowth, but can still be visited. They give an idea of how tl processing plant operated, thanks to guided tours offered by FAETEC The *salga* (salting) room where the meat was cured is still there and no serves as the Technical School's martial arts facility. The slaughterhou not only processed cattle, which came from neighbouring states and eve Argentina (known as "gringo cattle"), but other animals such as pigs ar poultry. In the garden, the large slaughterhouse generator can still be see It also produced energy for lighting the surrounding streets, making San

Cruz the first suburb to benefit fro electricity. The site had its own ra way station for the transport of fre meat. Today the abandoned static has been taken over by homele people, but, together with the rest the slaughterhouse buildings, it h been listed as a heritage site by tl municipality.

St Georges and the slaughterhouse

São Jorge is the city's most popular saint. On his feast day, 23 April, one of the biggest processions is in Praça Bodegão. For this occasion, the faithful throng the local streets on horseback, by horse and cart, or on foot. The procession has its origins in the stockbreeders from Minas Gerais who used to drive their cattle to the slaughterhouse.

PALACETE PRINCESA ISABEL ⑦

Home of the slaughterhouse director

Centro Cultural Municipal de Santa Cruz
Núcleo de Orintação e Pesquisa Histórica (NOPH) / Ecomuseu Santa Cruz
Rua das Palmeiras Imperiais
quarteirao.com.br – (21) 3365-4923
Tuesday to Friday 10am–6pm, Saturday 12pm–8pm (it is advisable to call
before coming to the cultural centre)
Train: Santa Cruz; Bus (BRT): Santa Cruz

The administration of the imperial slaughterhouse (see opposite) and the director's residence were located in the imposing Palacete do Matadouro, now known as Palacete Princesa Isabel. Also dating from 1881, the neoclassical building's gardens were designed by French urban planner François Marie Glaziou, who was responsible for renovating the Passeio Público (see p. 112). The enormous fig trees surrounding the palace are from this period, as are the imperious palm trees at the entrance. Shortly after its inauguration, it was converted into a school. Over the years, the building fell into disrepair and even caught fire. Since its restoration in the 1980s, it has housed a cultural centre and NOPH, a community initiative initially conceived to conserve historic buildings in Santa Cruz.

For the benefit of slaughterhouse employees and their families, a workers' village was built next to the palace.

Today the houses, although still occupied, are not what they once were.

The Santa Cruz Ecomuseum, originally known as the Ecomuseu do Quarteirão Cultural do Matadouro, is the city's first ecomuseum, a concept that originated in France in the 1970s. In these new "contemporary museums", the idea of "heritage" has replaced that of the "collection of objects" of traditional museums. Similarly, the notions of "participating community" and "terrain/sense of place" have taken over from "public/visitor" and "building/headquarters", respectively. The Santa Cruz museum was recognised in 1992 for NOPH's work, on the occasion of the first International Meeting of Ecomuseums held in Rio de Janeiro.

MARKER NUMBER 7 OF
THE ESTRADA REAL (ROYAL ROAD)

Route linking the imperial palaces of São Cristóvão and Santa Cruz

Opposite Paço Imperial de Santa Cruz
Praça Ruão
Train: Santa Cruz; Bus (BRT): Santa Cruz

© Rcandre

n the middle of the lawn at Praça Ruão, facing what was the Imperial Palace of Santa Cruz (now Battalion Villagran Cabrita, see p. 230), tands a modest stone marker. It is not far from a copy of the large vooden cross erected by the Jesuits in the 16th century. This is one of he 12 route markers of the Royal Road of Santa Cruz, which indicated he distance between the palaces of Santa Cruz and São Cristóvão.

According to researchers from the Núcleo de Orientação e Pesquisa Histórica (NOPH – Centre for Historical Orientation and Research) f Santa Cruz, the marker of Praça Ruão, which was not originally lo-ated here, is one of three still in existence. It also has something rather unique: you can read the symbols of the Empire and the Republic, re-pectively PI (Pedro I) and FN (Fazenda Nacional) and its number (7) nd a reference to the year 1826.

The other two known markers are number 11, also in Santa Cruz, n the square that bears its name; and number 10 at Paciência, near the 3RT bus terminal.

The route has existed since the time of the Jesuits – it was also known as the Jesuit Route. It connected Fazenda Santa Cruz to Morro lo Castelo (see p. 59), site of the Jesuit College. Over time, the route hanged its name: first, Caminho de Minas (as it went as far as Minas Gerais, where the gold sent to Portugal came from), and then Estrada Real, before becoming Estrada Imperial de Santa Cruz. Sections of the oute are now main city thoroughfares.

Dom Pedro I, his mistress and the origin of the name "paciência"

History and legend meet in the name of the railway station, opened in 1887, and the surrounding district – Paciência (Patience). This was the site of Fazenda do Mato da Paciência, probably the country's oldest sugar plantation. There is also evidence that when Dom Pedro I and his court were on their way to Santa Cruz palace (see p. 230), they stopped there to rest their horses.

The story goes that on reaching their resting place, the emperor mounted a waiting horse to join the Marquise de Santos (Domitila de Castro Canto e Melo, 1797–1867) from the nearby estate. His courtiers grew tired of waiting and kept asking the coachmen when they could resume their journey.

Knowing the habits of Dom Pedro and the time he spent in the arms of his famous mistress, the coachmen invariably replied: "Patience, patience, we must have patience..."

CAPELA MAGDALENA

A unique moment in a unique place

Estrada do Mato Alto 6024
contato_capelamagdalena@yahoo.com.br
(21) 99470-5431 – capelamagdalena@gmail.com
Visits on reservation only – avoid Friday evenings (massive traffic jams guaranteed, coming from Rio)
R$120 per person, including lunch or dinner, concert and entry to the museum

The Magdalena Chapel, an hour's drive from Rio city centre, towards the end of Barra de Tijuca, is unique.

The chapel, designed by Roberto de Regina, is also a concert venue, a restaurant and a small private museum of miniature reproductions of trains, planes, boats, castles, churches and famous buildings around the world.

Roberto, a former anaesthetist, is an amazing character. As he says himself, he's spent much of his life putting people to sleep. Now he wakes them up with his sensitivity, generosity and creativity. Indeed, he's done almost everything himself: painting frescoes on the chapel walls, building the harpsichord on which he gives concerts of Baroque music and designing most of the museum's 500 objects.

Although you can join an existing group (always call to book), we recommend getting together ten to twelve people (or more) to have the place to yourselves. In the words of "maestro" Roberto, who also prefers small groups, the conversation flows much better in an intimate setting.

Finally, for those for whom Renaissance music isn't an overwhelming passion, be assured that Roberto's spirit and the quality of the music will mean that you have a great time.

We strongly advise spending the whole day at the site: lunch at the Capela, then beach (Grumari or Guaratiba's secret beaches, see p. 238) and dinner nearby (such as the excellent Bira) or vice versa: beach for lunch, then dinner at the Capela. The renowned Burle Marx garden is another good and relatively nearby choice.

TRANSCARIOCA TRAIL TO THE WILD BEACHES OF GRUMARI

Deserted urban beaches

Trail starts at Barra de Guaratiba, Rua Siqueira Parlon
(21) 2410-1382 (Parque Natural Municipal do Grumari)
Distance: 8 km (one way, Guaratiba-Grumari round trip)
Duration: 4 hours (one way, Guaratiba-Grumari round trip)
Free

When dreaming of deserted beaches, the Caribbean or the Sout Pacific immediately springs to mind. But you don't need to g that far. Rio de Janeiro has five deserted beaches that are all accessibl

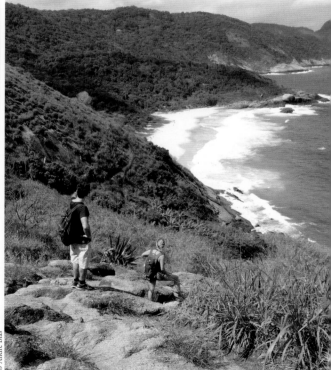

om the Transcarioca trail – its starting point coincides with the entrance to these beaches.

The path to the beaches of Búzios (not to be confused with the small easide town east of Rio), Perigoso, Meio, Funda and Inferno is easy and well-marked by wooden arrows interspersed with the yellow Transcarioca markers painted on trees and rocks. This signage, and the cleanliness f the beaches, are thanks to the efforts of the Grumari Municipal Natural Park managers and the NGO Amigos do Perigoso (Friends of Perigoso). They have adopted this stretch of the Transcarioca trail and regularly rganise volunteer clean-up operations to get rid of any rubbish.

During an expedition to Rio in 1833, the English botanist Sir Charles ames Fox Bunbury wrote: "The beaches near Rio are usually lined with ows of evergreen shrubs, mostly Cayenne cherry (Pitanga)...". Some wo centuries later, the wild beaches of Guaratiba haven't changed.

The walk alternates between closed forest sections (replanted in the 990s), rocky headlands and many white sand beaches. Don't forget to ake a hat, sunscreen and plenty of water.

Before reaching the first stretch of sand, a worthwhile detour (by a well-marked trail) to the Telegraph Mirador offers a spectacular view of Rio de Janeiro. After Praia do Perigoso, you can climb up to the path gain and resume your walk. The path, which goes round the headland, hen takes you to the beaches of Meio, Funda and Inferno. In fifteen ninutes you'll reach Praia do Meio, which has a freshwater spring. From here, carry on to the top of the hill at the far end of the beach. Another fteen minutes and you'll emerge at Praia do Funda, which is usually eserted. From there to Praia do Inferno, it's just a five-minute climb rom the headland.

After Inferno, follow the yellow markers to join the Transcarioca Grumari trail.

A stretch that ends at Grumari

After about 8 km, a stretch of the Transcarioca trail ends at Grumari. To get back to the starting point, you'll have to retrace your steps or travel by road between Grumari and Barra de Guaratiba.

If you prefer the second option, it's best to take two cars: leave one at the end of the trail and the other at the start, so that you can easily get back to the first.

It's said that when he needed to make difficult decisions, former Governor Leonel Brizola took a helicopter to Praia do Inferno to reflect in peace.

STATUE
OF A FOOTBALL PLAYER

Brazil's first football match

Rua Fonseca 240
Train: SuperVia at Central do Brasil, Bangu station

11

To the left of the main entrance of Bangu Shopping, near the ma
car park, is a bronze statue of a man holding a football, arm raise
in celebration. The inscription on the little fountain below claims this a
the site of Brazil's first football match.

This statue is a tribute to the Scot, Thomas Donohoe, who organised a six-aside match on 9 September 1894. The improvised pitch was on a vacant lot in front of the Fábrica de Tecidos Bangu (Bangu textile factory), with four stakes for goalposts. The reduced number of players was no problem for Donohoe and his teammates, nor was the absence of team jerseys or stopwatch. The point was to have a good time.

Donohoe, a dyer in a textile factory near Glasgow, Scotland, went to Rio de Janeiro in May 1894 to work in the new textile factory that had opened a year earlier. Arriving at Bangu, after an hour and a half's train ride from the centre of Rio, he found a town with only one street and less than a thousand residents. He also discovered that there were no football teams in the neighbourhood and that Brazilians knew nothing about the game – a disappointment for this 31-year-old athlete who'd been a keen player back home.

His family (wife and two young children) arrived at the port of Rio on 5 September 1894, with a special package for Donohoe in their luggage: a football. While still on the train to Bangu, Donohoe took something out of his suitcase that the other passengers thought was just a few strips of leather sewn together. To everyone's surprise, Donohoe pumped up the piece of leather into a ball and began to play with it right inside the carriage!

"Seu Danau", as he was called by the factory workers, defended the colours of Bangu Atlético Clube, which he'd helped to found in 1904. He died in October 1925.

The Bangu factory closed in February 2004, after decades spent playing a prominent role in the economic, social and cultural life of the region and of the city. Three years later, a commercial centre named Bangu Shopping restored the building's listed facade and opened for business.

As a result of Donohoe's improvisations and the lack of official rules (jerseys, stopwatch, goal markers, number of players, pitch dimensions) during the September 1894 match at Bangu, some consider that the country's first authentic football match was held in April 1895, seven months after Donohoe's, as it followed the Association Football rules set by Charles Miller from São Paulo.

BUMBA-MEU-BOI HOUSE/MUSEUM

Souvenir of Maranhão Bumba-meu-boi performances

Associação Raízes de Gericinó – Estrada do Gericinó 80, casa 3-A, Bangu
Daily, by reservation at (21) 3465-3959
Bus: 398, 366, 364, 2336 (Avenida Brasil stop – after the Coca-Cola
plant – take first street on right and walk about 150 m)

This small building with ornamental railings on its veranda, just at the entrance to an apartment block for around 300 residents, stands on a square of bare lawn. It's home to the small Bumba-meuboi museum (see opposite) and the headquarters of the non-profit association Raízes de Gericinó (Roots of Gericinó, a working-class district of Rio), born of the collective struggle for the right to home ownership in the Brazilian state of Maranhão.

The whole place is a living museum: apart from displaying the symbols and costumes used annually during local performances of Bumba-meu-boi, Raízes de Gericinó defends the cultural roots of the Maranhão region that persist in the neighbourhood. It offers clothing and accessories workshops, crafts, dance and reading for the children of the community, to preserve the Bumba-meuboi tradition.

Everything is informal but structured. The virtually family-run

roject goes back to the arrival in Rio of the Merces family from
Maranhão: Seu José, Dona Rosa and six of their children. Despite
he hard life endured by the poor migrants, the Merces liked to party
nd soon organised large gatherings with music from the Northeast
nd typical dishes. These events gradually won new followers in the
eighbourhood, families like themselves fighting for the ownership of
heir lodgings and to earn a living with dignity.

In 2011, homesick for Maranhão Bumba-meu-boi, the Merces held
heir first performance, which they called "Bumba-meu-boi, Star of
Gericinó". Gradually the group expanded beyond simple family ties.
he costumes and accessories, which had been brought from Maranhão,
vere now made by the community through the work of the Raízes
ssociation. Every year in July, the Star of Gericinó festival takes place in
he little square by the museum, amid music, dancing and many local
ishes.

What is Bumba-meu-boi?

Bumba-meu-boi, one of the richest representations of Brazilian folk-
lore, is widespread in the North and Northeast regions. Originating
in the 18th century, this performance – known by different names
in different states – is a kind of popular opera, fusing dance, music,
theatre and circus. The story is built around a rich farmer who owns
a splendid ox that is impounded and dies, but is resurrected. It all
ends in a huge party.

MUSEU BISPO DO ROSÁRIO

A genial "paranoid schizophrenic" artist

Estrada Rodrigues Caldas 3400
Jacarepaguá
(21) 3432-2402
museubispodorosario.com
Tuesday to Saturday 10am–5pm

Arthur Bispo do Rosário (1909–1989), a major figure of *art brut* ("raw" or "outsider" art), is certainly the artist whose work best reflects the approach of the great Brazilian psychiatrist Nise da Silveira (see Museu de Imagens do Inconsciente, p. 274). His creations are regularly shown in major exhibitions of international contemporary art.

In 1938, Bispo suffered a psychotic breakdown during which he became aware of his mission on Earth: recreating the universe in a form presentable to God to obtain redemption at the Last Judgment. He was

© Wilson Montenegro

arrested, hospitalised and diagnosed as a paranoid schizophrenic. He was finally admitted to Colônia Juliano Moreira, a psychiatric facility in Rio de Janeiro, where he remained until his death (see opposite). This artist, who never attended art school or even underwent occupational therapy (see below), has left behind a considerable body of 800 catalogued works in the museum that bears his name, opened in 2000.

He spent most of his life unwittingly exchanging ideas from his cell with the major currents of 20th-century art, from Marcel Duchamp's work on *arte povera* ("poor" art) through to conceptual art, at a time when Brazilian neoconcretism was breaking with all traditional media.

Bispo himself used mixed media. His works were created from found objects of everyday life, such as buttons, bottles, paper, cardboard, hospital sheets, various utensils, rubber boots or simple pieces of wood... His sculptures and other objects are sometimes covered with richly textured embroidered fabrics. He also made clothes such as his "Annunciation outfit" (the best known), which he intended to wear on Judgment Day, but also banners, boats, cars, a boxing ring and so on.

The museum has a policy of inviting contemporary artists to enter a dialogue with the work of Bispo de Rosário. This has resulted in a series of high-quality temporary exhibitions, justifying the addition of "Arte Contemporânea" to the museum's name.

Colônia Juliano Moreira: science, history and nature

Less than five minutes' drive from the museum, Colônia Juliano Moreira (Taquara district, 3400 Estrada Rodrigues Caldas, Jacarepaguá) is a psychiatric institution set up in the first half of the 20th century by Juliano Moreira (1873–1932), a pioneer of Brazilian psychiatry. He was known for his work on humanising treatment and rehabilitation through work, particularly on agricultural estates. With nearly 80 km^2 of protected grounds, the site still houses psychiatric units and a scientific campus inspired by the Institut Pasteur. You can discover many historical links as well as some exceptional natural surroundings. The premises are on the site of the former sugar plantation of Nossa Senhora dos Remédios (Our Lady of the Remedies), a Christian martyr who was dismembered in 1664. There's still a church of the same name (19th century), an 18th-century former aqueduct and many buildings that are unfortunately in poor condition. An enjoyable walk through the Parque Estadual da Pedra Branca (White Stone State Park) leads to Colônia's magnificent *cachoeira* (waterfall).

AÇUDE TRAIL

Cascatinha waterfall as you've never seen it before

Trail starts at junction of Estrada da Princesa Imperial and Estrada do Visconde do Bom Retiro (in Tijuca forest)
Duration: two hours
Museu do Açude: 764 Estrada do Açude, Alto da Boa Vista
(21) 98347-3429
Wednesday to Monday 11am–5pm (garden opens at 9am), free on Thursday

All Cariocas know Tijuca forest and have already heard of the Açude museum. What few know is that the two are connected by one of the most beautiful stretches of the Transcarioca trail. The path, which is maintained by the group of volunteers, is fully signposted with yellow markers that are the hallmarks of Transcarioca. The hike takes about two hours (starting near Os Esquilos restaurant and ending near Cascatinha) and is full of history, beautiful scenery and local wildlife.

The trail was used by Raymundo Ottoni de Castro Maya, former owner of the residence that is now the Açude museum, to reach Tijuca forest, which he managed from 1943 to 1947. Perhaps that's why it's so wide and well defined.

Between the forest and the museum, you'll pass through Alto do Cruzeiro, a place with a large wooden cross where Mass was held for the slaves in the days when the region was covered with coffee plantations. You can then climb up an observation tower and onto a bridge where, with luck, you'll spot toucans and hawks.

At Açude museum, you'll come across Castro Maya's former riding stables, nowadays home to a fantastic installation of artworks by Hélio Oiticica.

Continuing the walk for another hour or so is well worth the effort as you can visit Castro Maya's former residence – it's decorated with Portuguese *azulejos* that belonged to the Marquis of Marialva and has a Dutch fireplace carved at Pernambuco by Maurício de Nassau, among other fine works of art collected by Castro Maya. Even without going into the museum you can enjoy his garden, which is full of artworks and antique pots, along with modern installations acquired by the present management.

After rounding the main house and going through the stables, the Transcarioca climbs up again into Tijuca forest along a path that corresponds to the former boundaries of the property – you can still see markers with the initials CM (Castro Maya) stamped on them. Before heading down towards Praça Alfonso Vizeu, there's one last gem to be discovered: a wooden deck with the Cascatinha viewpoint. From there magnificent views of the forest open out – no traces of civilisation, just the green of the Atlantic forest surrounding the 30 m waterfall of Cascatinha de Taunay.

TRANSCARIOCA TRAIL, FROM ALTO DA BOA VISTA TO MESA DO IMPERADOR

360-degree views of Rio

Trailhead: Praça Afonso Viseu (Alto da Boa Vista)
Distance: 8.2 km (one way)
Duration: 3½ hours (one way)
Admission free
(21) 2492-2252, (21) 2492-2253 or (21) 3883-8800

This little-known trail connects the mountains of Tijuca and Carioc by the Morro do Queimado ridge. The lengthy, steep and tiring hike is still worth every drop of sweat but be sure to take plenty of wate with you. On the way, you'll pass a dozen watchtowers from where you can gaze down successively on Barra da Tijuca, Pedra da Gávea, the Zona Norte with Sierra dos Órgãos in the distance, Corcovado, Sugarloa Mountain and Rodrigo de Freitas lagoon, from various angles that only this trail can offer.

The route is fully signposted with yellow Transcarioca markers. The hike begins at the gate of Tijuca Forest National Park, Praça Afonso Viseu, in Alto da Boa Vista. Follow the yellow markers painted on poles cross Rua Boa Vista and ascend Rua Amado Nervo. Arriving at the na ional park gates, go into the forest by the wooden steps to the right. Be warned that it's a long climb through the Atlantic rainforest.

After about 40 minutes, you'll reach a fork in the track. To the right, about 10 minutes away, lies the viewpoint of Freira with its unrivalled panorama of Pedra da Gávea. The detour is well worth it.

Back on the main section of the Transcarioca trail, the climb continues and gradually offers the best views of the city.

After three hours' walk you'll reach the heights of Morro do Queinado, where the panorama is truly sublime. From this point, the trail is almost all downhill. It then continues through the forest and over a small hill before descending to a flat trail where you turn right.

You'll now find yourself following a former tram route opened in 1857 to link the botanical gardens and the city centre. The construction company dynamited half the route to widen it sufficiently for carriages to pass between the rocks, but work was never completed as the company went bankrupt.

Following the tram route, you'll reach the top of the steps leading to the Mesa do Imperador (Emperor's Table), where Dom Pedro II organised picnics with the royal family. From there, hardier souls can carry on as far as the Vista Chinesa (Chinese View) or the Solar da Imperatriz (Empress's Manor).

Otherwise we suggest taking two cars, leaving one at the Mesa do Imperador and the other in Praça Afonso Viseu, so you can easily get back to the first.

The mysterious inscription on Pedra da Gávea ⑯

At 842 m above sea level, Pedra da Gávea was the first Carioca mountain spotted by the sailors of the Portuguese expedition under Captain Gaspar de Lemos: on 1 January 1502 they saw the form of a topsail (*gávea*) and named the rock after it. For some, the theory (disputed) of the presence of Phoenicians in Brazil, is that Pedra da Gávea was shaped by Phoenician navigators who reached these shores around 1000 BC. According to a theory advanced by Robertus Comtaeus Nortmannus (1644) and George Horn (1652), the Phoenicians saw the outline of a sphinx in the rock. This theme was taken up in 1928 by the Austrian Ludwig Schwennhagen, who taught history and philosophy in Northeast Brazil, and especially by Bernardo da Silva Ramos, the "Brazilian Champollion", in 1930. This writer discovered inscriptions on the face of Pedra da Gávea in which he identified (and rendered in Portuguese) the Phoenician letters that compose, from right to left: TYRO PHENICIA, BADEZIR, PRIMOGÊNITO DE JETHBAAL (Phoenician of Tyre, Badezir, first son of Jethbaal). In 1954, Professor Henrique José de Souza, founder of the Sociedade Teosófica no Brasil (Theosophical Society of Brazil) came up with a revised version: "TYRO PHENICIA, JETHBAAL, PRIMOGÊNITO DE BADEZIR (Phoenician of Tyre, Jethbaal, first son of Badezir). Other people maintain that these letters are simply natural manifestations of weathered stone. Professor de Souza delved deep into the mystery of Pedra da Gávea and its relation to the Phoenician history of Brazil. According to him, the exiled king of Tyre (capital of Phoenicia), *Baal-Zir* or Badezir came here with his twin children *Yet-Baal-Bey* and *Yet-Baal-Bel*. (Some think the name Brazil is derived from Badezir, rather than from the national tree *pau-brasil* – *pau* meaning wood, and *brasil* meaning red/ember-like in Portuguese). One day, on the way across Guanabara Bay from Niteroi, their boat went straight to the bottom in a storm and they were all drowned. The bodies were recovered and placed at the heart of Pedra da Gávea (*Metaracanga* in the Tupi language), which in a way became their tomb. For millennia, the funerary remains rested inside the monolith in a cavity dug by human hands, and then mysteriously disappeared. The phrase "Phoenician of Tyre, Jethbaal, first son of Badezir" would then have been a posthumous tribute from the king Badezir to his elder son. It would have been the monarch's effigy carved on the face of Pedra da Gávea, in the guise of a bearded and helmeted old man. A huge white slab, rising up behind the Pedra on the São Conrado side, marks the supposed entrance to the interior of the monolith.

Tijuca – São Cristóvão – North

1. CENTRO MUNICIPAL DE REFERÊNCIA DA MÚSICA CARIOCA
   ARTUR DA TÁVOLA — *254*
2. *OMBRELLINO* OF SÃO SEBASTIÃO DOS CAPUCHINHOS — *256*
3. MUSICAL SIDEWALKS OF VILA ISABEL — *258*
4. THE FACE OF "BELLINI STATUE" — *260*
5. BAIRRO SANTA GENOVEVA — *262*
6. COLUNA DE PERSEPOLIS — *264*
7. ENTRANCE TO RIO ZOO — *266*
8. MUSEU DO SAMBA — *270*
9. BASÍLICA MENOR DO IMACULADO CORAÇÃO DE MARIA — *272*
10. MUSEU DE IMAGENS DO INCONSCIENTE — *274*
11. MUSEU DA VIDA — *276*
12. GUIDED TOUR OF PAVILHÃO MOURISCO — *278*
13. ASSOCIAÇÃO DE FERROMODELISMO DO RIO DE JANEIRO
    (AFERJ) — *282*
14. TREM DO SAMBA — *284*
15. MONTE ESCADA DE JACÓ — *286*
16. IGREJA DO BOM JESUS DA COLUNA — *288*
17. MARGAY CAT STATUE — *290*
18. CEMITÉRIO DOS PÁSSAROS — *292*
19. TUNNELS AND CAVES OF PARQUE DARKE DE MATTOS — *294*

CENTRO MUNICIPAL DE REFERÊNCIA DA MÚSICA CARIOCA ARTUR DA TÁVOLA

Rio's home of music

Rua Conde de Bonfim 824
(21) 3238-3831
centrodamusicacarioca.cultura@gmail.com
Thursday to Saturday 10am–8pm Sunday 10am–6pm
Metro: Uruguai

From Tijuca's Praça Saens Peña, heading up Rua Conde de Bonfim towards the Usina or Alto da Boavista neighbourhoods, there's a surprise in store at the corner of Rua Garibaldi. Here, in contrast to the monotonous succession of buildings and commercial establishments bordering most of the route, an ancient and imposing French-style medieval mansion stands out.

This small palace, built in 1921, is one of the few examples of its kind left in the neighbourhood. It was designed by the architect Gaspar José de Souza Reis as the home of Portuguese merchant Manoel Vieira Júnior. It was subsequently owned by an Italian called Mário Bianchi, a successful businessman in the transport sector.

Although the building's architectural beauty leaves no one indifferent, it has not always been so. Neglected for over twenty years, the fabric of the building began to deteriorate. Its prospects started to improve in the late 1980s, when a group of residents and regulars of the Bar da Dona Maria (traditional samba venue, opposite the mansion) launched a campaign to have the building listed before converting it into a cultural centre devoted to music. The initiative was successful and in 1995, Palacete Garibaldi was listed as local heritage. After long and extensive renovations, the Artur da Távola Municipal Centre for Carioca Music moved there in June 2007. This space is intended to preserve the city's rich musical heritage.

The ground-floor rooms are reserved for exhibitions, workshops and concerts of classical music. The floor above is reserved for the administration. Besides its verandas and balconies, the place also has a welcoming winter garden and beautiful stained-glass doors and windows.

In addition to the original mansion, the centre has the use of two annexes built during the renovations: a concert hall with a capacity of 161 seats, a small administration building and three rooms for workshops and music lessons.

A former garage houses a recording studio and three additional workshops. Finally, there's a pretty garden with a little jetty at the far end: a reminder of the time when the Maracanã river was clean and navigable.

OMBRELLINO OF SÃO SEBASTIÃO DOS CAPUCHINHOS

The forgotten symbol of basilicas

Rua Haddock Lobo 266
(21) 2204-7900
Daily 8am–8pm
Metro: Afonso Pena

To the right of the altar of the basilica church of St Sebastian of the Capuchins, the discreet canopy resembling an umbrella, whose wooden frame is covered with striped red and yellow silk in the colour of the Vatican Pontifical government, is known as an umbraculum or *ombrellino*. These colours have themselves been inherited from ancien

Rome, where they were those of the Roman Senate.

Historically, the canopy was a tent that sheltered the patriarch and royalty in the Old Testament. The symbols of canopy and bell (tintinnabulum) are reserved for basilicas and signify their link with the pope. The canopy is half open when in a minor basilica (as here) and fully open in major basilicas (see below and *Secret Rome* in this series of guides). During papal visits, however, it is also fully open in minor basilicas.

What is a basilica?

In the Roman Empire, the basilica was the palace where the king (*basileus*) dispensed justice. After the Edict of Milan (313) that brought Christians out of hiding and put an end to persecution, Emperor Constantine had four churches built in Rome, known as "major" basilicas, which he donated to the pope. These are St Peter's in Vatican City, on the supposed site of the martyrdom of St Peter; St Paul Outside the Walls, on the scene of the martyrdom of St Paul; St Maria Maggiore, the first church in Christendom dedicated to Mary; and St John Lateran, in honour of the apostle "whom Jesus loved". The Archbasilica of St John in the Lateran is the seat of the pope and the Cathedral of Rome, "mother and head of all the churches of the city and the world". All other basilicas in Rome or elsewhere are classified as "minor": they have privileges such as the protection of the Holy See linked with one of the four major basilicas. Nowadays a church can be honoured with the title of basilica by papal decree, according to its spiritual influence and exemplary daily practices.

Three major relics of Rio de Janeiro at St Sebastian's

By a decision of Pope Francis on 1 November 2015 (commemorating the date of the last Mass in São Sebastião do Castelo church, demolished in 1922 along with the *morro* of the same name – see p. 59), São Sebastião dos Capuchinhos became a minor basilica, to highlight its important role. It houses three of the city's major relics previously kept in São Sebastião do Castelo church – the city's foundation stone from 1565 (left of the nave); the remains of the city founder, Estácio de Sá, who died in 1567 (in front of the altar); and the historical image (1563) of St Sebastian, patron saint of the city (see p. 119). Every year on 20 January (St Sebastian's feast day), this image joins the procession to the Catedral Metropolitana in the city centre. The rest of the year, the image is not on public view.

MUSICAL SIDEWALKS OF VILA ISABEL

A musical neighbourhood

Vila Isabel
Boulevard 28 de Setembro (from Praça Maracanã to Praça Barão de Drumond)
Bus: from Zona Sul (432, 433, 438, 439); Centro (222, etc.)

The musical sidewalks of Vila Isabel – inaugurated in 1964 by Governor Carlos Lacerda as part of preparations for the commemoration of the city's fourth centenary the following year – are found on both sides of the main thoroughfare, Avenida / Boulevard 28 de Setembro. They are an ode to Brazilian popular music: engraved on the black and white Portuguese paving are the scores of various popular songs plus images of instruments.

The project was the brainchild of architect Orlando Magdalena, a local resident, and met with the enthusiastic approval of the authorities. The musical scores were divided into pages to match the width of the sidewalks, and drawings of instruments such as the guitar, *cavaquinho* (small Portuguese guitar), piano and *pandeiro* (percussion) were dotted among them. Another architect, Hugo Ribeiro, helped to design these instruments and paid tribute to Noel Rosa, songwriter, singer and guitar or mandolin player, by affixing his initials to a guitar. The choice of songs was made by the creator of the project and Almirante, a renowned expert in Brazilian popular music.

The series of songs, twenty in all, starts with the city's anthem, *Cidade maravilhosa* (*Marvellous City*) by André Filho, in Praça Maracanã. Among the others are *Ó abre alas* (the "abre alas" is the lorry opening the Carnaval parade) by Chiquinha Gonzaga, the first song composed for the carnival; *Pelo telefone* (*By Telephone*) by Donga and Mauro de Almeida, the first recorded samba (1918); *Feitiço da Vila* (*The Charm of Vila*) by Noel Rosa, composer *par excellence* of Vila Isabel and leading light of 1930s Brazilian popular music; *Ave Maria* by Erotildes Campos and Jonas Neves, in front of Nossa Senhora de Lourdes basilica; *Jura* (*Oath*) by Sinhô and J. B. Silva; and *Carinhoso* (*Affectionate*) by Pixinguinha and Antônio da Rocha Viana. The last song is *Renascer das cinzas* (*Reborn from the Ashes*) by Martinho da Vila, in Praça Barão de Drumond. The musical sidewalks were listed by Rio City Hall in April 1999.

There is another tribute to Brazilian music at Vila Isabel: a statue of Noel Rosa in Praça Maracanã, at the entrance to the neighbourhood. Noel Rosa is shown sitting on a bar stool with a cigarette between his fingers, a waiter in attendance. On the table beside him stand a bottle of beer, a glass and a sheet, also in bronze, bearing the words of the samba *Conversa de botequim* (Bistro Conversation). Beside him, an empty chair invites visitors to sit down for a selfie. A curious feature of the statue is that the young man's features are based on those of Rosa's father. Unveiled on 22 March 1996, it was designed by Joás Pereira Passos from Paraíba state.

THE FACE
OF THE BELLINI STATUE

Statue with different features to its namesake

Gate D of Mário Filho stadium (Maracanã)
Rua Professor Eurico Rabelo
Metro: Maracanã

In front of the Maracanã stadium's gate D stands the statue of Bellini
Hilderaldo Luiz Bellini, a Brazilian footballer of Italian origin, was
captain of the national soccer team when Brazil won its first World

Cup in Sweden in 1958. Although the Maracanã statue is named after him, not many people know (or even notice) that its features bear not the slightest resemblance to Bellini.

Most of those involved in this episode are now dead, so it's difficult to explain what happened. In a 2010 interview, the player's widow recalled that her husband had twice asked for the sculptor Matheus Fernandes "because of his athletic stature and the position of his hand".

Some people argue that the statue's face is that of singer Francisco Alves, aka "King of the Voice", who was very popular in the 1950s. But it also bears a strong resemblance to journalist Hamilton Sbarra, who in an interview with a newspaper at the time revealed that the sculptor had asked him for a photo, saying he needed "a face with a Graeco-Roman profile, like mine". Although suspicious, Sbarra complied.

The inscription on the base of the statue (9 m tall and weighing 3 tonnes), which was unveiled on 13 November 1960, makes no reference to Bellini but is simply dedicated "To the World Champions". But over time, people started to refer to it as the "statue of Bellini" and that's what everybody calls it now.

The difference between the official and popular versions of events seems typical of this stadium, named after journalist Mário Filho but known worldwide as the Maracanã, or "Maraca" to keen Carioca fans. It was built for the 1950 World Cup and opened on 16 June of that year, with a friendly match between the Rio de Janeiro and São Paulo teams in which the first goal was scored by the Carioca player Didi. Top scorer at the Maracanã is Zico, idol of the Flamengo club: 333 goals in 435 games. Pelé scored his thousandth goal there too, in 1969.

Macaranã is a word of Tupí origin, meaning "like a *chocalho*" (the sound of birds of the Psittacidae subfamily *maracana*, which includes species such as parrot, macaw and parakeet). Before the stadium was built, the site was home to numerous bird species.

The stadium was once the largest in the world (for the final of the 1950 World Cup, it hosted over 199,000 spectators, many standing). It is still the largest in Brazil, with a capacity of 78,800 (all seated).

BAIRRO SANTA GENOVEVA

A mini-Montmartre in Rio

Rua São Cristóvão 446
Visits only on invitation from a local resident (ask at the entrance) or
during Mass (very irregular)
Metro: São Cristóvão

An attractive gate alongside number 446 Rua São Cristóvão bears the inscription "Bairro Santa Genoveva". If you're lucky enough to meet a resident at the gate, and they agree to "invite" you to visit his private neighbourhood, you'll have the privilege of strolling around a group of a hundred little houses built by the Viscount of Moraes. Leader of the Portuguese colony in Brazil, Eurico José Pereira de Moraes established this workers' village on a small *morro* in 1917 close to the Persian column in front of the Conde de Linhares Military Museum (see p. 264).

Although the area has the reputation of being a small Montmartre, it is rather a small St Geneviève (Santa Genoveva). The Montagne Sainte-Geneviève in Paris, a hill on the Left Bank, is, as here, much smaller than Montmartre.

The most charming spot is right at the top of the *morro*, where a small square and an attractive tree overlook a church that is only open on the last Saturday of the month. The church, a scaled-down copy of Sacré-Cœur (Basilica of the Sacred Heart in Montmartre, Paris), was built to fulfil a promise made by the viscount to the patron saint of Paris (St Geneviève) concerning his wife's health.

All the streets in the neighbourhood (Rua Savero, Rua Geronia, Praça Nanterre, Rua Lutécia, etc.) refer to St Geneviève: born in Nanterre near Paris in 423, she was the only daughter of Severus (Savero), a probably Romanised Frank, and Géroncia (Geronia), a woman of Greek origin. Paris was known as Lutèce in St Geneviève's time.

COLUNA DE PERSEPOLIS

Forgotten column of Persepolis

Praça Pedro II
São Cristóvão
Metro: São Cristóvão

he column in Praça Pedro II, at the end of Rua São Cristóvão, opposite the entrance to Conde de Linhares military museum, often goes unnoticed.

The 9-metre-high column was a gift from Iranian President Mahmoud Ahmadinejad on the occasion of the 2012 Rio climate change conference. It is a replica of a column that still stands in one of the throne rooms (*apadana*) at Persepolis – once a capital city of the Achaemenid Persian empire and now a UNESCO World Heritage site. The city was founded in 521 BC by the Persian King Darius the Great, long before the Muslim era.

The column is surmounted by two opposing bull's heads. In the Persian tradition, this animal is an image of strength and power, protection and defence, and a personification of royal authority.

At the foot of the column, two bas-reliefs show a lion devouring a bull. In Persian tradition, this scene symbolises the New Year (Nowruz, between 20 and 22 March, the spring equinox), when the constellation Leo is in the zenith, while that of Taurus heads south. Nowruz marks the beginning of agricultural activity after the winter period.

Finally, an inscription in English and Portuguese recalls a dialogue between King Darius and Ahura Mazda, the Zoroastrian god worshipped in Persia before the introduction of Islam. Zoroastrianism is still practised in Iran and parts of India. Note the translation error in the Portuguese version of this dialogue, which recalls the benefits of virtuous conduct: *desejo que, se ele fizer o mal, que ele não seja punido* ("I wish that he who does evil should not be punished"). The phrase should be the other way round (English version is correct).

ENTRANCE
TO RIO ZOO

The gift of an English duke in artificial stone

Parque Quinta da Boa Vista
Metro: São Cristóvão

Not much attention is paid to the entrance to Rio Zoo (Jardim Zoó logico). Yet it's the only South American example of Coade stone, a artificial construction material of English origin (see opposite).

This gateway was the gift of General Hugh Percy, 2nd Duke of North umberland, for the marriage of Dom Pedro I and the future empres Maria Leopoldina of Austria (1817).

John Johnston, the English architect responsible for the renovation o São Cristóvão palace at the time, set the gateway at the entrance of wha became the Imperial Palace, as seen in the engraving below. It remaine there until at least the 1860s before being moved to the zoo.

The gateway is a copy of a Robert Adam design that graces Syo House, the Duke of Northumberland's former residence on the outskir of London.

See overleaf for more illustrations of the former site of the São Cristóvão gateway and of Syon House.

The mystery of Coade stone

Coade stone (Lithodipyra or "twice-fired stone"), little known outside the UK, is a ceramic "artificial stone" named after Eleanor Coade junior (1733–1821).

The material owes its success to the property boom that London was experiencing at that time. As most buildings were of brick, the architects made wide use of Coade stone to embellish their facades. The mix contains finely ground, fired potters' clay that can be cast very easily to produce statues, architectural decorations and garden ornaments, allowing very fine detail and exact copies.

The moulds can be used over and over again, greatly reducing manufacturing costs.

Another important advantage of Coade stone is its extreme durability. It is resistant to the elements and the corrosive urban air – examples over 200 years old still show no obvious signs of wear or deterioration.

Eleanor was both a brilliant businesswoman and a very fine sculptor, so she not only ran one of the most successful 18th-century companies but she also created many of the original sculptures from which the moulds were taken. It was thought that Eleanor took her secret Coade stone recipe to her grave, but in recent years a few potters have managed to crack the formula. Today, there are an estimated 650 Coade stone sculptures around the world. The vast majority can be found in Great Britain (see *Secret Edinburgh* from the same publisher). Some can be found in the United States and Canada. The only one in South America is the one from Rio.

Former site of the São Cristóvão gateway

The Imperial Palace of São Cristóvão was built in 1803 by the Portuguese merchant Elias Antonio Lopes.

He donated it in 1808 to the Prince-Regent D. João VI when the entire court fled Portugal. The palace later became the residence of the emperors of Brazil.

The two engravings below show how it looked in days gone by, without the Coade stone portal.

Syon House gateway (United Kingdom)

Syon House has been owned by the Dukes of Northumberland since 1594.

Located on the outskirts of London, the building and its grounds were built in the 16th century on the site of the medieval Syon Abbey. The gate of which the entrance to Rio Zoo is a copy frames one of the entrances to the vast estate, which covers no less than 80 hectares.

MUSEU DO SAMBA

Everything you ever wanted to know about samba

Avenida Visconde de Niterói 1296
Visits by appointment on (21) 3234-5777
contato@museudosamba.org.br – museudosamba.org.br
Bus: 402, 665

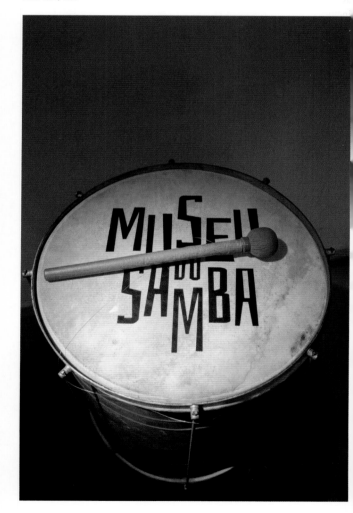

The Samba Museum is located at the foot of Mangueira district, home to the Estação Primeira de Mangueira (one of the city's most traditional samba schools), in a hangar that was abandoned until 2003, when it was sold to the museum for renovation.

The museum tours are led by researchers who introduce the exhibitions and give information about little-known aspects of samba and its major figures. For those who want to dig deeper, we recommend asking for the Vivência do Samba (Living the Samba) programme: this includes the guided tour, a samba workshop with players and dancers, and the opportunity to try on Carnaval costumes and eat *feijoada* (bean and meat stew) prepared by a Mangueira resident.

The museum has several permanent exhibitions, such as Samba Patrimônio Cultural do Brasil, which presents the history of samba and honours its protagonists. In addition to explanatory texts (in Portuguese) and photographs, it includes costumes donated by the *sambistas*. There are also displays entitled Simplesmente Cartola (Cartola, Quite Simply) on the life of the famous Angenor de Oliveira, known as Cartola, one of the founders of the samba school in 1928, and another on Dona Zica da Mangueira e do Brasil, Cartola's wife. She was a leading female figure in the Mangueira samba school and neighbourhood.

Looking round the exhibitions and chatting with the guide, you'll learn such things as the reason for the Mangueira colours of green and pink – not because Cartola was a supporter of Fluminense Football Club, as many think, but because these are the colours of the Carnaval dance group of his childhood, Arrepiados, from Laranjeiras.

In the same vein, the museum has a lot more information on samba and the samba schools. Apart from the exhibitions, it has a collection of over a hundred testimonies by sambistas and researchers. It also runs courses and workshops in addition to the *rodas* (concerts) organised every second Friday of the month in a large graffiti-covered space that mimics the *favela* ambience.

BASÍLICA MENOR DO IMACULADO CORAÇÃO DE MARIA

The city's only neo-Moorish church

Rua Coração de Maria 66
(21) 99947-9009 o((21) 2501-4574
pascombicm@gmail.com
Monday to Friday 6.30am–11am and 6.30pm–8pm, Saturday and
Sunday 6.30am–8pm
Every second Saturday of the month, at 2pm, a traditional Latin
(Tridentine) Mass – during which the priest always faces the Blessed
Sacrament and may turn his back to the congregation – is held at the altar
dedicated to the Sacred Heart
Train: Méier

Five minutes' walk from Méier station in the north of the city, the spectacular Minor Basilica of the Immaculate Heart of Mary is the only neo-Moorish Roman Catholic church in Rio and one of the few in the country. Definitely worth a visit.

Although the church was built between 1909 and 1917 by the monks of the Consecration of the Missionary Sons of the Immaculate Heart of Mary, the tower was not completed until 1924. The design was by Adolfo Morales de Los Rios, the Spanish architect responsible for some of the city's most iconic buildings, such as the early 20th-century National Museum of Fine Arts.

Behind the two doors in carved rosewood, the impressive interior is in typical neo-Moorish style with coloured mosaics, *azulejos* decorating the walls, and stained glass with a profusion of geometric details, colours and shapes, such the petals of a rose.

The Méier basilica, which can seat 900 people, is highly sought after for weddings because of its great beauty. Listed by the prefecture in 2009, the building features in a series of postcards from the *Olhos de ver* (Eyes to See) collection launched in 2012 by the city prefecture's Instituto Rio Patrimônio da Humanidade.

One of Rio's six roman catholic minor basilicas

The other five are those of the Imaculada Conceição in Botafogo, Nossa Senhora de Lourdes in Vila Isabel, São Sebastião dos Capuchinhos in Tijuca (see p. 256), Nossa Senhora de Penha in Penha and Santa Teresinha do Menino Jesus in Tijuca.

This special status is granted by the pope to churches that stand out as a place of pilgrimage and are known for their liturgical zeal, historical significance or architectural and artistic beauty.

Pope John XXIII granted the title of minor basilica to the Méier church in 1964.

MUSEU DE IMAGENS
DO INCONSCIENTE

A must for those who love art brut *and research into the subconscious*

Instituto Municipal Nise da Silveira
Rua Ramiro Magalhães 521
(21) 3111-7467
Tuesday to Saturday 10am–4pm
Bus: 238 and 239

The Museum of Images of the Subconscious was founded in 1952 by psychiatrist Nise da Silveira (1905–1999) to conserve artwork roduced in the occupational therapy workshops she had set up.

The life of this exceptional woman, the subject of Roberto Berliner's 015 film *Nise: O coração da loucura (Nise: The Heart of Madness)*, is ifficult to sum up. The only woman among 157 men at the University f Bahia, she was accused of communism during the years of the Var- as dictatorship when she came to work in Rio de Janeiro, imprisoned, nen banned from practising for eight years. She rebelled against new sychiatric treatments such as electroshock and lobotomy, refusing to se them, and in 1946 opened a therapeutic occupational service at the edro II Psychiatric Centre (now Instituto Municipal Nise da Silvei- a). Painting and modelling workshops were set up where the patients occupied" their own workspaces – as can still be seen today. Here the nmates, mostly chronic schizophrenics whom da Silveira called her "cli- nts", were offered a new form of expression and psychiatric treatment. Despite being in open conflict with her colleagues, she received support nd recognition from personalities such as eminent Swiss psychiatrist :arl Gustav Jung and leading Brazilian art critic Mário Pedrosa.

Pedrosa was instinctively convinced of the talent of some of da Sil- eira's "clients". He wrote reference works on what he called "virgin art", similar concept to French artist Jean Dubuffet's, who coined the term *rt brut* to describe the creations of people with no formal artistic back- round. Pedrosa even wanted to bring the artworks to Rio's Museum f Modern Art but met with strong opposition from da Silveira, who anted to keep them in "her" museum near the workshops where they ere made.

The museum has collected about 350,000 pieces over the sixty years f its existence, some of which have been shown at over 100 exhibitions orldwide.

The occupational therapy workshops continue and some of the "cli- nts" exhibit their work alongside internationally recognised names: ok out for Emygdio de Barros, Adelina Gomes, Isaac Liberato, Carlos erthuis and Fernando Diniz, among others.

MUSEU DA VIDA

Science is life

Fundação Oswaldo Cruz (Fiocruz)
Avenida Brasil 4365
(21) 2598-4242
museudavida.fiocruz.br
Tuesday to Friday 9am–4.30pm and Saturday 10am–4pm, tours in Portuguese
only
Admission free
Taxi recommended

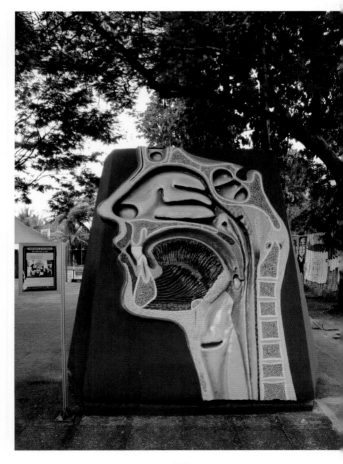

ocated on the Oswaldo Cruz Foundation (Fiocruz) campus, with 35,000 m² of green space, historic buildings and scientific research nstallations, the Museum of Life runs many unusual activities around he theme of the human body.

The museum, which opened on 25 May 1999, also has a small butterfly house colonised by four species from the Americas.

The guided tours present the life of butterflies, providing minute letails of their life cycle and eating habits, and the secrets behind their aried colours and survival strategies. Sometimes butterflies settle on he visitors.

A variety of games and experiments on microscopic or macroscopic ives and the perception of light and sound are also offered in the Biodiscovery Hall. You can examine a giant model of the human eye and, under the direction of the guides, learn how images are formed.

Microscopes are provided for children and adults to observe the workshop of the micro-world" of insects and human tissues. It's also very interesting to try making models of cells with the materials supplied, which you're sometimes allowed to take home.

Through experiments and interactive games, visitors aged 9 and bove can learn about the role of physics in the explanation of certain phenomena: how can vision be deceptive, making us perceive a movement instead of a static image?

How is it possible to see colours where there was previously only black and white?

GUIDED TOUR
OF PAVILHÃO MOURISCO

A captivating neo-Moorish building

Fundação Oswaldo Cruz (Oswaldo Cruz Foundation – Fiocruz)
Avenida Brasil 4365
(21) 2598-4242 – portal.fiocruz.br
Visit included with admission to the Museu da vida
Check the museum calendar at museudavida.fiocruz.br
Admission free
Access by taxi recommended

On the way from Galeao International Airport to the Zona Sul, five to 10 minutes from the airport, you'll notice an imposing building on the horizon to the right: the beautiful Moorish Pavilion is the headquarters of the Oswaldo Cruz Foundation. Built between 1905 and 1918, it is listed as national heritage. Contrary to what you might think, it is open to the public.

The building was designed by Dr Oswaldo Cruz (1872–1917), a noted physician and epidemiologist, and is one of Brazil's very few neo-Moorish monuments.

It uses a harmonious blend of materials from many countries: the bricks, tiles and stuccowork are French, the marble originally from Italy, the *azulejos* Portuguese, the lighting fixtures German, the metalwork English, including the beautiful staircase, the windows Belgian and the woodwork Brazilian. The elevator, installed in 1909, is the oldest still operating in the city.

The bathrooms on all floors are stacked in a tower, accessible from the building but not part of the main construction, to avoid any cross-contamination.

The pavilion contains mysteries that feed the imagination of those who work there or visit. There is talk of footsteps or strange noises at night when everyone is gone; doors slamming even when they're closed; and a book that someone is looking for spontaneously appearing right in front of them. Not to mention the story of the night guard on his rounds, who went to the third-floor library at dawn and found a man dressed in white sitting there. The terrified guard collapsed before making a run for it.

The surrounding area was a swamp (now filled in), which is why the area is called Manguinhos, meaning "little swamp".

The hidden floor

Seen from the outside, the building appears to have four floors. In fact there are five – there's another before the top floor, windowless (designed as a darkroom), which is why you would never guess it was there. Photographer J. Pinto worked there from 1903 to 1946 to record the production of serums and vaccines, in addition to his research and teaching activities.

The splendid reading room of the rare books collection

On the third floor of the building, the rare books section of the library is a magnificent space, fully preserved, with dark-brown Brazilian walnut (*imbuia*) wood furniture, cast iron and bronze light fittings, with German made accessories in lilac opal. The wooden flooring consists of geometric shapes in various shades, the walls and ceiling feature pretty ornaments in white plaster.

The collection includes works from the 17th century, such as the first treatise on the natural history of Brazil by Willem Piso and Georg Marggraf, *Naturalis historia brasiliae*, dating from 1648. The reading room is open to visitors, but only researchers are allowed to consult the books.

ASSOCIAÇÃO DE FERROMODELISMO DO RIO DE JANEIRO (AFERJ)

Model railway in an abandoned station

Rua Francisco Eugênio – Room 106, ground floor
Visit on appointment: aferj.ho@gmail.com – Saturday 9am–5pm (admission free)
Metro: São Cristovão

The model railway track is one of Rio's great secrets. Every Saturday, from about 9am to 5pm, the 30 members of the Model Railway Association of Rio de Janeiro can indulge their passion. They run their miniature locomotives and wagons around a network that has about 300 m of track over a 55 m² surface.

The association, which was set up in 1986, also has a small repair workshop for members. They pay R$150 each to register and R$30 per month for the right to operate their little trains.

The venue is open to the public and members are usually delighted to share their enthusiasm with visitors who drop in.

You'll learn that the circuit has five different tracks, each independent from the other: once the train is on the network, the only thing the operator can change is its speed. And, as in real life, they'll run a high-speed train faster than a freight train.

When will Brazil have a proper railway network?

Originally developed to support a coffee-driven economy, the Brazilian rail passenger network today is almost non-existent. The only viable stretch is between Belo Horizonte and Vitoria, far from being the country's most essential route.

In a country that frequently suffers from apocalyptic traffic jams on the way out of the major cities, this lack of trains (even to connect the main cities) is a scandal.

The quality of life is at stake. And it's an urgent question for the country.

TREM DO SAMBA

Contagious joy

Every year, first Saturday in December: first train for guests leaves at
6.04pm, followed by four others at 20-minute intervals
Central do Brasil station to Oswaldo Cruz
tremdosamba.com.br
Admission free

The fantastic Samba Train, inaugurated in 1996, is a project of singer and composer Marquinhos from the Oswaldo Cruz neighbourhood: he wanted to commemorate National Samba Day and restore the

former glory of this traditional musical genre. These trains run once a year in the early evening of the first Saturday in December, to mark National Samba Day, which is celebrated on the 2nd of the same month.

The day of festivities begins in an atmosphere of contagious joy at Central Station, with a great free show around midday. On the way to Oswaldo Cruz (30 minutes by train), a different samba band plays in each carriage.

On arrival, the musicians perform for free on stage or during more informal *rodas de samba* shows, in bars or on the street corners of this district considered the mecca of traditional Carioca samba.

A concert inspired by the Fête de la musique *in Paris*

Oswaldo Cruz concerts started in the second year of the Samba Train, when Marquinhos learned of the music festival held every 21 June in Paris, and felt that there was nothing better than samba musicians to greet the arrival of the train.

Why 6.04pm?

The first Samba Train for invited guests, with Marquinhos and representatives of the old guard of Rio's traditional samba schools, always starts at 6.04pm in memory of the fact that, in the 1930s, it was the train that Paulo da Portela caught every day on his way home. During the trip, Paulo and his friends sang and played, taking advantage of the lack of police repression at a time when the samba was banned. After the 6.04 train, four others leave Central Station, one every 20 minutes.

Paulo da Portela, real name Paulo Benjamin de Oliveira (1901–1949), singer and composer, was a founder of the Portela samba school – both him and the school were named after the nearby Portela road. Paulo, a major figure of Brazilian culture, fought hard to change the preconceptions surrounding the samba players, depicting them as thugs and vagabonds rather than respected artists. For example, he insisted that the local people should be dressed in the samba school colours on parade day.

MONTE ESCADA DE JACÓ

A place of powerful spiritual energy?

Avenida Mons Felix 512
24/7
Mass Mondays at 9am
Metro: Irajá

One of the most astonishing places in Rio lies at the heart of the Zona Norte, a few minutes' walk from Irajá metro – the Mount of Jacob's Ladder, a reference to the episode in the Old Testament.

Until 2010, the hillside was the haunt of prostitutes and the place (known as the "microwave"...) where traffickers from the surrounding *favelas* came to "liquidate" anybody who would get in their way.

All this changed on 15 May 2010, when God appeared in a dream to Father Marcelo Flores, of the Igreja Evangélica Assembléia de Deus (Evangelical Church of the Assembly of God), commanding him to transform the site into a place of spirituality. Following this dream, Father Marcelo opened his Bible at the passage describing Jacob's ladder (see below), and named the hill accordingly.

With the help of friends, Father Marcelo, who lives nearby, cleaned up the site (which belongs to the army) and began to paint the stones white. Verses from the Bible were added to some of them.

From then on, this became one of Rio's most fervent prayer and meditation venues. Depending on the time of day (busiest Monday morning and Friday evening, as well as Saturday evening and Sunday afternoon), you'll meet people praying alone or in groups, kneeling facing the city, quietly reading the Bible, or others, more active, who come along to chat with other believers.

Although the site is mainly frequented by Evangelists, other denominations are also welcome.

The biblical story of Jacob's ladder

Jacob's dream is an episode of the Book of Genesis (28: 10–19) that begins as follows: "Jacob left Beersheba, and set out for Harran. When he reached a certain place, he stopped for the night because the sun had set. Taking one of the stones there, he put it under his head and lay down to sleep. He had a dream in which he saw a stairway resting on the earth, with its top reaching to heaven, and the angels of God were ascending and descending on it."

IGREJA DO BOM JESUS DA COLUNA

A forgotten colonial gem

Cidade Universitária – Ilha do Fundão
(21) 3836-8199
Mass on Sunday at 10am
Admission free
Access: private car or taxi

© Halley Pacheco de Oliveira

The church of Good Jesus of the Column, built in 1705 according to the inscription on the cloister door, is a real colonial gem with national heritage status. Built as part of a Franciscan convent, the church is out in the countryside on a military range (to reach it, you have to pass through a control point – ID needed), with beautiful views over Guanabara Bay.

Like one or two of Rio's other splendid ecclesiastical buildings – the Benedictine Abbey of Our Lady of Montserrat, more commonly known as the Mosteiro de São Bento; and Lapa dos Mercadores, the Traders' Church of Our Lady of Lapa – the church has a narthex (enclosed porch at the entrance). Between the bell tower and the sacristy, on the right, the cloister corridor has two floors topped by arches (all that's left of the convent).

The interior of the church is notable for the simplicity of its smooth walls, but the main and side altars are late Rococo in style. Facing the chapel is the richly decorated stele of Antônio Teles de Menezes and his descendants, the former owners of the land ceded to the Franciscans (the same family that built the Arco de Teles on the site of the old pillory in Praça XV).

In the crypt, in front of the ossuary of the Teles de Menezes family, is a secret passage that allowed the monks to escape to a part of the island protected by rocky outcrops in case of an attack from the sea – a sort of emergency exit leading to a cove. Enemy ships could easily be spotted from the church, which enjoyed a wide view of Guanabara Bay.

It was in this church that the feast day of St Francis of Assisi was celebrated, which is why João VI was a frequent visitor to the island when he lived in Brazil. After independence, the government took over the island and the convent dependencies were used as a lazaretto, a hostel for immigrants and a barracks. Then in 1868 an asylum, now abandoned, was built closer to the sea (Asilo dos Inválidos da Pátria) for the wounded soldiers of the Paraguayan War. The church has been luckier and continues to attract worshippers, mostly soldiers.

The church of Bom Jesus da Coluna was built in the 18th century on what was then Ilha do Bom Jesus, part of a small archipelago of eight islands. In the early 1950s the embankment that links all the islands was completed and extended to Fundão, about 3 million m², to accommodate the Federal University of Rio de Janeiro (UFRJ). The site now houses major research and technology centres.

MARGAY CAT STATUE

The maracajá *of Paranapuã*

End of Guanabara beach
Ilha do Governador
Bus: 634

On Governor's Island off Guanabara beach, a statue of the *maracajá*, the Indian term for the wild cats that existed in the 16th century, stands on Pedra da Onca (Jaguar rock), which owes its name to the statue because of the marked similarity between the *maracajá* (margay or tiger cat) and the jaguar. The rock was also known as Pedra dos Amores (Lovers' rock).

The statue is said to have been inspired by a legend, which started with a young woman from the island's Temiminó tribe who had a pet *maracajá.* Every afternoon she took it to the beach and dived from the rock, while the wild cat watched her.

One day, the legend goes, she was drowned and the *maracajá* waited for her on the rock until it died. Like any legend there may be no truth in it, but it has inspired the local people. In the 1920s, they decided to build a monument to immortalise this story, symbol of friendship, loyalty and hope.

A local artist, Guttman Bicho, designed the concrete cat that was later installed on the largest of the rounded rocks at the end of Guanabara beach. The statue crumbled over time, so on 20 January 1965, the feast day of St Sebastian, patron of the city (see p. 127), it was replaced by another which still stands there today.

Despite the pollution in the bay, the site of the statue is exquisite: on one side, a small wooded area and, on the other, a little beach frequented by swimmers and fishers.

The view is superb: as well as the panorama over the bay, you can see in the distance the peak of Dedo de Deus (Finger of God), the mountainous area of Teresópolis.

Ilha do gato

While the indigenous people called the place Ilha de Paranapuã (meaning "round sea"), the Portuguese, until the late 1560s, knew it as Ilha do Gato (Cat Island), perhaps in reference to the large numbers of *maracajá* living there. The name Ilha do Governador only appeared in 1567 after Mem de Sá, governor-general of the Portuguese colony, handed over much of the island to his great-grandson Salvador Correia de Sá (appointed governor of the captaincy of Rio de Janeiro in 1568).

Where does the name of Galeão Airport come from?

Another governor, Salvador Correa de Sá e Benevides, installed a shipyard on the island that in 1663 built the Galeão Padre Eterno, considered at the time to be the largest ship in the world. The site remained known as Ponta do Galeão (galleon), which subsequently gave its name to the international airport.

CEMITÉRIO DOS PÁSSAROS

The world's only known bird cemetery

Rua Manoel de Macedo
Ilha de Paquetá
Boats to Paquetá throughout the day from Praça XV, downtown Rio
Timetable and fares at grupoccr.com.br/barcas/linhas-horarios-tarifas

In the quiet Rua Manoel de Macedo, next to Paquetá cemetery, is a burial ground for birds, the only one in the world. The handful of graves are all identical: the tradition is that owners of dead birds check the available space among the graves (over time, the bodies decompose into the earth), and there they lay to rest the creature that kept them company during its lifetime.

Modern legislation on the protection of wild life means that fewer and fewer people keep wild animals in captivity, which is why there is a reduction in the number of "funerals". But since its establishment by local artist Pedro Bruno (1888–1949), in addition to being a cemetery, this wooded and serene area is also an ode to the love of nature, as residents will confirm.

As well as the tombs and two monuments – *The shot bird* and *Landing of the tired bird* – one wall has short poems by well-known and unknown writers. The cemetery also has seats and little tables, which are very popular in this neighbourhood meeting place.

Brazil's first nudist club

Paquetá is the second largest island in Guanabara Bay. It has also given its name to an archipelago of 18 islands and *matações* (rounded rocks that look like small islands). In the 1950s, the controversial Brazilian artist Luz del Fuego (1917–1967) set up the country's first nudist club on the island of Sol.

How can you be sure of your partner's love?

Paquetá and its many nicknames, such as the Island of Love or the Pearl of Guanabara, have inspired several romantic traditions. To be sure of your partner's love, go to the Pedra dos Namorados (Lovers' Rock), at the tip of Praia José Bonifácio, and throw three small stones, from behind you, on top of the rock, while thinking about your great love. If at least one of them stays up on the rock, then your passion is mutual. And if you want to find love, just sip the water of São Roque well and someone on the island will succumb to your charms.

Since 1967, Paquetá has had ten trees listed by municipal decree. In addition to a baobab, there are almond, mango, tamarind and jackfruit.

TUNNELS AND CAVES
OF PARQUE DARKE DE MATTOS

Signs of kaolin mining

Ilha de Paquetá, at the end of Praia José
Bonifácio
Daily 8am–5pm
Admission free
Boats to Paquetá throughout the day from Praça XV, downtown Rio
Timetable and fares at grupoccr.com.br/barcas/linhas-horarios-tarifas

At the end of José Bonifácio beach, on the beautiful island of Paquetá, Darke de Mattos park offers visitors stunning views of the bay, ancient trees and unusual tunnels and caves which are the remains of kaolin mines (a type of white clay used in making porcelain). Although this is a 20th-century park with lawns and a children's playground, it's also a fine example of the Romantic landscaped garden that was much in vogue in the 19th century.

Paths lead to the top of the small Morro da Cruz (Hill of the Cross) and its belvedere. Most of the caves resulting from the clay excavations can be found along these paths. They are all shapes and sizes: while some are large enough to enter, they're dark inside, so it's not a good idea to venture in alone and without a light.

At the far end of the park, a boardwalk offers a stunning view of the bay, with Ilha do Governador (Governor's Island) in the distance. Nearby, at a slightly higher level, is perhaps the most surprising feature of the gardens: a short tunnel dug in the hillside which opens onto a small and pretty beach – for children, it's like discovering an uninhabited island. Horses are often to be seen on the beach, which is near the stables of the horses that pull the traditional Paquetá carts.

Although there was once a thriving farm in the region, it closed in 1747. Later, the Jesuits made porcelain with the clay from the hill and, at the end of the 19th century, a weaving mill was in operation here.

The land was purchased in the early 20th century by the entrepreneur Darke de Mattos, who had a large house built with a pool and a hangar for the seaplanes he piloted. All this has disappeared. His daughter donated the property to the prefecture, which converted it into a park.

Prince Regent Dom João often went to Paquetá. His first visit, in late 1808, came about quite by chance when his ship ran aground during a wild storm on one of the island's beaches. Despite turning up so unexpectedly, he enjoyed a warm welcome. Dom João returned there again and again and, during one of his stays, he was presented with a set of china made from the local clay.

1st Batalhão de Engenharia de Combate 230

80-tonne doors 223

1908 Exposição Nacional: from "pestilential" to "marvellous" city 188

Academia Brasileira de Literatura de Cordel 156

Açude trail 246

Agricultural estate of Santa Cruz 231

Another Ipanema tribute to Bahia's independence heroes 211

"Ao Rei dos Mágicos" building 34

Aqueduct, spring, fountain, plaza, street: the importance to Rio of the Carioca 129

Arezzo's stained-glass window 38

Art Deco details of the Tribunal Regional do Trabalho 58

Associação de Ferromodelismo do Rio de Janeiro (AFERJ) 282

Azulejos at the Clube dos Democráticos 109

Bairro Santa Genoveva 262

Ball from the first match in the Brazililan team selection 139

Bas-reliefs at the Centro Administrativo do Tribunal de Justiça 73

Bas-reliefs by Orestes Acquarone 36

Bas-relief of the Associação Comercial do Rio de Janeiro (ACRJ) 20

Bas-relief statue of São Sebastião 118

Basílica Menor do Imaculado Coração de Maria 272

Biblical story of Jacob's ladder 287

Biblioteca Escolar Municipal de Copacabana Carlos Drummond de Andrade 163

Brazil's first abstract sculpture 147

Brazil's first nudist club 293

Bugle boy statue 210

Bumba-meu-boi house/museum 242

Capanema hanging gardens 48

Capela de Nossa Senhora da Cabeça 198

Capela Magdalena 236

Casa Franklin facade 98

Casa Marajoara 136

Cemitério dos Pássaros 292

Centro Municipal de Referência da Música Carioca Artur da Távola 254

Centro Cultural do Movimento Escoteiro 18

Centro Nyingma de Boudismo Tibetano 216

Ceramics at the Ministério da Fazenda 60

Chapel only open for Mass on Mondays and the Day of the Dead 146

Christ statue of Igreja Santa Cruz dos Militares 22

Coffee route 196

Colônia Juliano Moreira: science, history and nature 245

Coluna de Persepolis 264

Copacabana Batcave 166

Copacabana's first skyscraper 179

Cross that gave its name to a neighbourhood 231

Curse of Teatro João Caetano 104

Di Cavalcanti frescoes on the newsroom 86

Di Cavalcanti panels at the João Caetano theatre 100

Djanira, the artist who didn't want to be known as such 41

Dom Pedro I, his mistress and the origin of the name "paciência" 235

Entrance to Rio zoo 266

Entrance to the Academiea Imperial de Belas Artes 202

Escola de música concert hall 110

Esotericism of the Brazilian flag 206

Estação de Hidroaviões staircase 66

Exposição internacional do Centenário do Brasil 52

Eyes of the clock 65

Facade of the former Lambert perfume and soap factory 92

Face of the Bellini statue 260

Fig tree in Rua Faro 199

First skyscraper on Avenida Rio Branco 36

"For the English to see ..." 85

Former course of the Carioca river 128

Former site of the São Cristóvão gateway 268

Former Vatican embassy in Rio 151

Foul smell that led to the park being renovated 113

Foundlings' wheels, Carmelite Convento de Santa Teresa 154

Gávea route markers 204

General Osório's riding gear 30

Getúlio Vargas memorial 120

Golden Rose of the Museu Arquidiocesano de Arte Sacra 106

Gonçalves Dias medallion 37

Graveyard of the "little angels" 142

Gruta de Lourdes, Igreja da Santissima Trindade 130

Guahy building 176

Guided tour of Academia Brasileira de Letras 50

Guided tour of Forte São José 192

Guided tour of Pavilhão Mourisco 278

Hangar do zeppelin 222

Hidden floor 281

Hiking at Morro da Babilônia 182

Historic library 81

How can you be sure of your partner's love? 293

How do we know about St Emerentiana? 29

"If he'd done the same in Italy, he'd have been an internationally renowned architect" 125

Igreja de Nossa Senhora do Bonsucesso 64

Igreja do Bom Jesus da Coluna 288

Igreja Santa Cruz de Copacabana 164

Ilha do gato 291

Instituto Cultural Cravo Albin 190

Inverno statue in the Passeio Público 112

Itahy building 170

Itaóca building 174

Lagarto fountain on Rua Frei Caneca 90

Library of the Museu Histórico Nacional 72

Liceu Literário Português azulejos 42

Lobby of Edifício Petrônio 178

Manuel Luiz Osório 31

Margay cat statue 290

Marker number 7 of the Estrada Real 234

Medaillon of Edifício Brasília 43

Memorial commemorating the opening of the ports in 1808 122

Mestre Valentim at the Botanical Garden 203

Minister who wanted a modern building 49

Monte escada de Jacó 286

Monument to the Carioca river 126

Morro da Viúva 133

Morro de Babilônia at Cannes 183

Mosaic by Lygia Clark 162

Motor race that inspired a March of the Rio carnaval 205

Muiraquitãs: Amazonian amulets 175

Museu Bispo do Rosário 244

Museu da Bíblia 99

Museu da Polícia Civil waxworks 94

Museu da Polícia Militar do Estado do Rio de Janeiro 91

Museu da Vida 276

Museu de Imagens do Inconsciente 274

Museu do Corpo de Fuzileiros Navais 16

Museu do Samba 270

Museu Histórico e Diplomático of the Palácio Itamaraty 80

Museu Judaico do Rio de Janeiro 44

Musical sidewalks of Vila Isabel 258

Mysterious inscription on Pedra da Gávea 251

Mystery of Coade stone 267

Napoleon's lock of hair 160

Obelisk to mark the widening of Avenida Atlântica 180

Observatório do Valongo 78

- 297 -

Occult significance of Morro Dois Irmãos ... 208

Ombrellino of São Sebastião dos Capuchinhos ... 256

One of Rio's six Roman Catholic minor basilicas ... 273

Opening of the ports in 1808 ... 123

Orestes Acquarone ... 36

Origin of the expression "Cidade maravilhosa" ... 189

Origin of the word *carioca* ... 128

Other reminders of the 1922–1923 Expo ... 53

Oval panels by Leandro Joaquim ... 68

Paintings in the nave of Igreja Nossa Senhora da Candelária ... 19

Palacete Princesa Isabel ... 233

Palácio episcopal and fortaleza da Conceição ... 82

Palácio Guanabara ... 140

Parque do Martelo ... 218

Parque Estadual de Chacrinha ... 165

Parque Natural Municipal da Catacumba to Humaitá trail ... 214

Pavement dedicated to Carlos Drummond de Andrade ... 161

Ponte dos Jesuítas ... 228

Portinari panels at Palácio Gustavo Capanema ... 46

Projeto Morrinho ... 148

Raised floor of Igreja do Santíssimo Sacramento da Antiga Sé ... 96

Rare neo-Egyptian building ... 76

Razing of Morro do Castelo to make way for Esplanada Castelo and one of Rio's centres of Art Deco ... 59

Remains of a fountain recalling the viceroy's forbidden love ... 113

Remains of Morros do Inhangá ... 168

Remains of the Academia Imperial de Belas Artes ... 103

Remains of the Santa Teresa cable car ... 153

Rent-a-slave for an evening at the theatre ... 105

Right arm of Nossa Senhora dos Prazeres' statue ... 95

Rio: a city built on land largely reclaimed from the sea ... 56

Rio de Janeiro, capital of Latin America Art Deco ... 172

Roxy staircase copies ocean liner ... 177

Ruins of the Imperial slaughterhouse ... 232

Russian orthodox Church of St Zinaida ... 152

Santa Barbara e as Operarias ceramic panel ... 40

Santa Luzia car-park wall ... 54

Seaview ... 113

Secrets of Igreja de São José ... 32

Secrets of the Instituto Histórico e Geográfico Brasileiro ... 114

"Senta a Pua" memorial ... 226

Shell in the Igreja de Nossa Senhora da Lapa dos Mercadores ... 26

Slab of concrete from Galeão runway that Pope John Paul II kissed ... 107

Sociedade Budista do Brasil ... 150

Sophisticated statue ... 49

Splendid reading room of the rare books collection ... 281

St Georges and the slaughterhouse ... 232

Stained-glass windows at Fluminense football club ... 138

Stained-glass window commemorating the navy dead ... 146

Staircase at the Museu de Ciências da Terra ... 186

Stairway of the former Ministry of Finance ... 62

Station with dozens of copies of Brazilian rocks ... 167

Statue of a football player ... 240

Statue of Chopin ... 184

Statue of João Caetano ... 102

Statue of São Dismas ... 88

Statue of St Emerentiana ... 28

Statue of the *orixá* Ossanha ... 200

Stretch that ends at Grumari ... 239

ugar loaves at the National
istorical Museum   70

ymbols of the passion at Igreja
anta Cruz dos Militares   24

yon House gateway   269

"hese are human remains!"   85

hree major relics of Rio de
aneiro at St Sebastian's   257

radentes' historic cell   14

o live happily, live hidden   162

omb of the Marquis of Paraná   144

ain inspired by the *Fête de la
usique* in Paris   285

anscarioca trail, from Alto da
oa Vista to Mesa do Imperador   248

anscarioca trail to the wild beaches
f Grumari   238

em do samba   284

unnels and caves of Parque Darke
e Mattos   294

wo airships and a bicycle   224

nfinished painting of Pedro II's
oronation   115

ase of the Triumph of Galatea by
rançois Girardon   212

eronica's veil, an extraordinary
nd little-known relic   25

Vestige of the Exposition of 1922   51

Viewpoint that throws light on Morro
do Castelo   61

Villino Silveira doorway   124

Wallace fountain   229

What is a basilica?   257

What is Bumba-meu-boi?   243

What is a foundlings' wheel?   155

What is the Golden Rose?   107

When will Brazil have a proper
railway network?   283

Where does Galeão airport's name
come from?   291

Where does the name Fonte da
Saudade come from?   217

Where does the name Morro da
Viúva come from?   134

Where does the word "cordel"
come from?   157

Why 6.04pm?   285

Why was Chopin's statue placed
in front of the Municipal Theatre
in 1951?   185

World's largest port of entry for
slaves   84

Thomas Jonglez

It was September 1995 and Thomas Jonglez was in Peshawar, the northern Pakistani city 20 kilometres from the tribal zone he was to visit a few days later. It occurred to him that he should record the hidden aspects of his native city, Paris, which he knew so well. During his seven-month trip back home from Beijing, the countries he crossed took in Tibet (entering clandestinely, hidden under blankets in an overnight bus), Iran and Kurdistan. He never took a plane but travelled by boat, train or bus, hitchhiking, cycling, on horseback or on foot, reaching Paris just in time to celebrate Christmas with the family.

On his return, he spent two fantastic years wandering the streets of the capital to gather material for his first "secret guide", written with a friend. For the next seven years he worked in the steel industry until the passion for discovery overtook him. He launched Jonglez Publishing in 2003 and moved to Venice three years later.

In 2013, in search of new adventures, the family left Venice and spent six months travelling to Brazil, via North Korea, Micronesia, the Solomon Islands, Easter Island, Peru and Bolivia.

After seven years in Rio de Janeiro, he now lives in Berlin with his wife and three children.

Jonglez Publishing produces a range of titles in nine languages, released in 40 countries.

ACKNOWLEDGEMENTS

Serge Cajfinger, João Roberto Marinho, Roman Carel, Andrea Carel, Elaine de Souza Carrilho, Miro, Sergio, Susi Cantarino, Rodrigo Garcia, Pauline Dufresne, Thibaut Dufresne, Viviane Hentsch, Carmo Mineiro, Jovelino Mineiro, Marie-Laure Jousset, Hubert Jousset, Deborah Bertrand, Damien Bertrand, Corinne Tisserand, Didier Tisserand, Jérémy Leclerc, Marie Gervais, Sébastien Gervais, Marie Héger, Olivier Héger, Joaquim Monteiro, Jaqueline Sinesio, Alix de Ligne, Daniel Mello, Observatorio do Valongo, Charlotte Valade, Marcio Roiter, Romulo Fialdini, Milena Manfredini, Marc Pottier, Raquel Fernandes, Gabriela Carrera, Luiza Mello, Wilson Montenegro, Delphine Moulin, André Blas, Helio Brasil, Helena Cristina Duarte Cordeiro, Angela Cristina Duarte Souza, Major João Rogério de Souza Armada, Charles Siqueira, Genival André, Padre Enrico Arrigoni, Ricardo Cravo Albin, Vagner Machado, Cristiane Machado, Claudia Rose Ribeiro, José Queiroga, Mario Chagas, Rita Santos, Sidney Silva, Valquiria Cabral, Auricélia Mercês, Walter Priosti, Odalice Priosti, Fábio Lázaro, Rogéria Villete, Rosângela Mansur, Márcio Pinto de Oliveira, Tania Mara Araújo, Jorge Mario Jauregui, Magda Beatriz Vilela, José Lavrador, Helena Celestino, Marquinhos de Oswaldo Cruz, Vera Dias, Paulo Knauss, Frei Cassiano Gonçalves, Tenente Rodrigo Moura Visoni, Adriana Bandeira, Mario Carlos Lopes, Fabio Iglesias, Haendel Gomes, Heliton Barros, Nilcemar Nogueira, Desiree Reis, Dhaniel Cohen, Osvaldo Rezende, Luiz Eugenio Teixeira Leite, Federico Rodriguez, Claudia Guerra, Paulo Knauss, Luiz Williams, Joe Berardo, Pedro Aguilar, Janice Melhem Santos, Eliana Kruzicevic, Marcelo Conde, Carlos Fernando de Andrade, Ronald Pimentel, Aloysio Neves, Luiz Claudio Kastrup, José Carvalho.

PHOTO CREDITS

Thomas Jonglez: Museu do Corpo de Fuzileiros Navais, Centro Cultural do Movimento Escoteiro, Paintings in the nave of Igreja Nossa Senhora da Candelária, Bas-relief of the Associação Comercial do Rio de Janeiro (ACRJ), Christ statue of Igreja Santa Cruz dos Militares, Symbols of the passion at Igreja Santa Cruz dos Militares, Shell in the Igreja de Nossa Senhora da Lapa dos Mercadores, Statue of St Emerentiana, General Osório's riding gear, Secrets of Igreja de São José, Gonçalves Dias medallion, *Santa Barbara e as Operarias* ceramic panel, Liceu Literário Português *azulejos*, Museu Judaico do Rio de Janeiro, Guided tour of Academia Brasileira de Letras, Santa Luzia car-park wall, Ceramics at the Ministério da Fazenda, Igreja de Nossa Senhora do Bonsucesso, Estação de Hidroaviões staircase, Oval panels by Leandro Joaquim, Sugar loaves at the National Historical Museum, Library of the Museu Histórico Nacional, Bas-reliefs at the Centro Administrativo do Tribunal de Justiça, Rare neo-Egyptian building, Observatório do Valongo, Museu Histórico e Diplomático of the Palácio Itamaraty, Di Cavalcanti frescoes on the newsroom, Statue of São Dismas, Lagarto fountain on Rua Frei Caneca, Museu da Polícia militar do Estado do Rio de Janeiro, Facade of the former Lambert perfume and soap factory, Museu da Polícia Civil waxworks, Right arm of Nossa Senhora dos Prazeres' statue, Raised floor of Igreja do Santíssimo Sacramento da Antiga Sé, Casa Franklin facade, Museu da Bíblia, Di Cavalcanti panels at the João Caetano theatre, Statue of João Caetano, Escola de música concert hall, *Inverno* statue in the Passeio Público, Secrets of the Instituto Histórico e Geográfico Brasileiro, Bas-relief statue of São Sebastião, Getúlio Vargas memorial, Memorial commemorating the opening of the ports in 1808, Villino Silveira doorway, Monument to the Carioca river, Gruta de Lourdes, Igreja da Santissima Trindade, Morro da Viúva, Casa Marajoara (right page), Stained-glass windows at Fluminense football club, Graveyard of the "little angels", Stained-glass window commemorating the navy dead, Sociedade budista do Brasil, Russian orthodox Church of St Zinaida, Foundlings' wheels, Carmelite Convento de Santa Teresa, Academia Brasileira de Literatura de Cordel, Napoleon's lock of hair, Pavement dedicated to Carlos Drummond de Andrade, Igreja Santa Cruz de Copacabana, Parque Estadual de Chacrinha, Obelisk to mark the widening of Avenida Atlântica, Hiking at Morro da Babilônia, Staircase at the Museu de Ciências da Terra, Instituto cultural Cravo Albin, Guided tour of Forte São José, Coffee route, Capela de Nossa Senhora da Cabeça, Entrance to the Academiea Imperial de Belas Artes, Gávea route markers, Occult significance of Morro Dois Irmãos, Bugle boy statue, *Triomphe de Galatée* vase by François Girardon, Parque do Martelo, Hangar do zeppelin (first page on the left), Capela Magdalena, Centro Municipal de Referência da Música Carioca Artur da Távola, *Ombrellino* of São Sebastião dos Capuchinhos, Face of the Bellini statue, Associação de Ferromodelismo do Rio de Janeiro (AFERJ), Bairro Santa Genoveva (left page), Coluna de Persepolis, Entrance to Rio zoo, Museu da Vida, Guided tour of Pavilhão Mourisco, Hidden floor, Trem do samba, Monte escada de Jacó

Elsa Leydier: "Ao Rei dos Mágicos" building, Capanema, Capanema hanging gardens, Palácio episcopal and fortaleza da Conceição, Golden Rose of the Museu Arquidiocesano de Arte Sacra, Statue of Chopin, Centro Nyingma de Boudismo Tibetano, Cemitério dos Pássaros, Tunnels and caves of Parque Darke de Mattos

Charlotte Valade: Casa Marajoara (left page), Tomb of the Marquis of Paraná, Biblioteca Escolar Municipal de Copacabana Carlos Drummond de Andrade, Copacabana Batcave, Guahy building, Museu do Samba, Basílica Menor do Imaculado Coração de Maria

Marcio Roiter: Art Deco details of the Tribunal Regional do Trabalho, Curse of Teatro João Caetano, Itahy building, Rio de Janeiro, capital of Latin America Art Deco, Lobby of Edifício Petrônio
Romulo Fialdini: Arezzo's stained-glass window

Cartography: **Cyrille Suss** – Layout: **Emmanuelle Willard Toulemonde** – Translation: **Caroline Lawrence** – Copy-editing: **Jana Gough and Matt Gay** – Proofreading: **Olivia Fuller** – Publishing: **Clémence Mathé**

© JONGLEZ 2025
Registration of copyright: January 2025 – Edition: 02
ISBN: 978-2-36195-844-2
Printed in Bulgaria by Dedrax